To Be or Not To Be

Is That The Question?

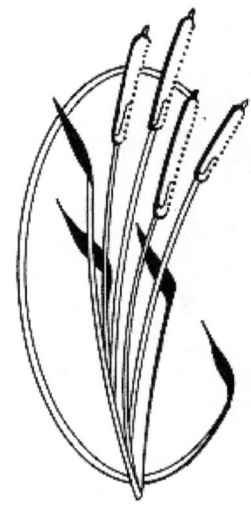

To Be or Not To Be

Is That The Question?

By Reverend

Gregory L. Williamson

Senior Publisher
Steven Lawrence Hill Sr.

Awarded Publishing House
ASA Publishing Company
Established Since 2005

A Publisher Trademark Cover page

ASA Publishing Company
Awarded Best Publisher for Quality Books 2008, 2009
105 E. Front St., Suite 205, Monroe, Michigan 48161
www.asapublishingcompany.com

All Rights Reserved. No part of this publication may be reproduced, stored in a retrieval system or transmitted in any form or by any means electronic, mechanical, photocopying, recording, taping, web distribution, information storage, or otherwise, without the prior written permission of the publisher. Author/writer rights to "Freedom of Speech" protected by and with the "1st Amendment" of the Constitution of the United States of America. This is a work of religious educational learning purposes. With this title page, the reader is notified that this text is an educational tool, and the publisher does not assume, and expressly disclaims any obligation to obtain and/or include any other information other than that provided by the author. Any belief system, promotional motivations, including but not limited to the use of non-fiction characters and/or characteristics of this book, are within the boundaries of the author's own creativity and/or testimony in order to reflect the nature and concept of the book.

Any and all vending sales and distribution not permitted without full book cover and this title page.

Copyrights©2012 Reverend Gregory L. Williamson, All Rights Reserved
Book: To Be or Not To Be *"Is That The Question?"*
Date Published: 01.31.12
Edition: 1 *Trade Paperback*
Book ASAPCID: 2380591
ISBN: 978-1-886528-18-5
Library of Congress Cataloging-in-Publication Data

This book was published in the United States of America.
State of Michigan

A Publisher Trademark Title page

Table of Contents
TO BE OR NOT TO BE *IS THAT THE QUESTION?*

Acknowledgement .... (i)

Introduction .... (a)

Chapter 1   *The Purpose To Be* 1

Chapter 2   *The Call To Be* 20

Chapter 3   *The Place To Be* 37

Chapter 4   *The Decision To Be* 50

Chapter 5   *The Need To Be* 65

Chapter 6   *The Challenge To Be* 77

Chapter 7   *The Way To Be* 95

Chapter 8   *The Mind To Be* 113

Acknowledgement

If you are currently reading this book, I want to first thank you for allowing me to share with you what God has shared with me. For too many years I struggled with balancing my efforts with God's requirements and have constantly come up short. Finally, I discovered that I was indeed a born again follower of Jesus Christ, but I was caught up in the web of "legalism." I have since discovered that an unbelievable number of other Christians are as well. Legalism is a tactic of the devil and can be very destructive as it relates to your Christian maturity.

Legalism is built largely on pride and a huge set of rules that masquerade as Godly expectations that feed into pride. Legalism proposes a scorecard that says, if I obey all of God's commandments and don't commit a sin today, I am a good Christian. When I make mistakes (get angry, sin, do the wrong thing, think the wrong thoughts), I am not a good Christian and don't deserve God's grace and mercy. That much is true, we can never deserve God's grace or mercy.

Legalism encourages you to compare your efforts to others. Therefore, if you do less wrong than your brother, you score higher and are in a closer relationship and higher acceptance with God. How foolish! I now see. It is impossible to live a perfect and infallible life through our own efforts. This is what I was attempting to do in my walk with Christ, and it's what so many other Christians are attempting to do.

Philippians 4:13 tells us that we can do all things through Christ who strengthens us. When we yield our will to God, He performs the work, and the results are attributed to us. If we fail to yield to Him, we attempt to do the work, and He allows us to, and most of the time we fail. After discovering that my success is not based on my effort but on God's, I now have peace with my struggles and power in my strategies. I discovered this through a plethora of connections and encounters.

My *motivation to put my thoughts in book form* came from Pastor Jake Gaines. The i*nformation* was simply by the direction of God. My *inspiration* comes from the teaching I received from the late Pastor Alvin Hawkins and Pastor Billy D. Allen of Liberty Baptist Church – Pontiac, Michigan, my two Pastors; Eric Burr and Anthony Pettus Sr., and the many speakers from the Mountain Top Conference (MTC) held in Midland Michigan. Only God could bring these mighty men of God into my life at the right time. It was just what I needed to become all that I am in Christ today. I want to briefly introduce you to these great men that have had such a positive influence on my life.

Kelvin Burton - Dr. Kelvin Burton is a doctor of medicine as well as a Minister of the gospel. In addition to his profession, he Pastors Christian Comforters Church in Georgia. Dr. Burton addresses the importance of physical and spiritual health. You might hear Dr. Burton pointing out that, as it relates to men's health, we should not follow Paul's advice in I Corinthians 11:28, "But let a man examine himself." He points out that too many people have insurance packages that they never use and too many are dying prematurely because when they seek help, it's too late. He assured us that from the physical perspective, we can't examine ourselves. We need to be examined by a physician.

Dr. E. L. Branch – Dr. E. L. Branch is Pastor of Third New Hope Church in Detroit, Michigan. My experience with Dr. Branch has been more from a student's perspective. I have been a part of revivals, lectures and conferences where he was a presenter. In each instance I found his teaching to be penetrating to the soul. I will always remember the valuable words of advice he offered to my Pastor, "Walk in your God-given authority." I think that is great advice for us all.

Haman Cross – Pastor Haman Cross, Jr., is Pastor of Rosedale Park Baptist Church in Detroit, Michigan. He is one of the most relevant Pastor, Teacher, Speaker and men I have ever met. I only know Pastor Cross as a speaker/lecturer at the MTC, but he is one of the speakers that the conference attendees deliberate with great anticipation. Pastor Cross brings it in a way like no other: straight, with no chaser. If you are a man and can't understand Pastor Cross, you probably need to "Man-UP."

Craig Ester - Dr. Craig Ester is an Assistant Pastor at New Prospect Baptist Church in Detroit, Michigan. Dr. Ester has a compelling commitment to the development of men and women with great focus on supporting their

Pastors. He speaks to the vital importance of an effective Armor Bearing ministry each year at the Mountain Top Conference (MTC) in Midland, Michigan. Dr. Ester not only brings practical biblical examples to support his presentation, he lives it out in his own ministry.

Jake Gaines – Pastor Jake Gaines pastors Synagogue Missionary Baptist Church in Detroit, Michigan. Pastor Gaines is one of the most humble leaders in the gospel ministry that I have ever met. He sacrifices his time two Saturdays a month for the development of men through bible study. His scholarly approach and dedication to God's word is impeccable. I equate his acumen with that of Socrates, who said in essence, "Wisdom is knowing that you don't know everything." I attribute my motivation for writing this book to Pastor Jake Gaines.

Everett Jennings – Pastor Everett Jennings is the Senior Pastor of Providence Baptist Church in Detroit, Michigan. He is a MTC presenter for the Pastor's and Minister's sessions. Although I don't know Pastor Jennings on a personal level, his presentation of God's word is unmatched. Each year, Pastor Jennings challenges Pastors, Ministers and Laymen to stand up and be the powerful, authoritative, influential, spirit-filled and spirit-led men that God has called us to be.

Gabriel Lewis – Pastor Gabriel Lewis is Pastor of Gabriel Lewis Ministries and one of the most unique men I have ever met. God gave Pastor Lewis an extraordinary ability to reach unsaved men and to develop them into Christian men. It is no wonder that men in ministry gravitate to him. His down-to- earth and right-to-the point teaching style hits you, and he is not ashamed to let you know that in some instances, he was there, too, at some point in his life. I've never had a conversation with Pastor Lewis and not grown from it.

Ellis Liddell – Mr. Ellis Liddell is the president of ELE Wealth-Management in Southfield, Michigan. I met Mr. Liddell at one of his financial meetings in Southfield several years ago. I heard about him through a talk radio program, "Inside Detroit," hosted by Mildred Gaddis. Since then, I have entrusted ELE with my personal investment strategies. Mr. Liddell has been one of our conference speakers since its inception.

James Minnick – Pastor Minnick is Pastor of Mount Pleasant Missionary Baptist Church in Detroit, Michigan. Pastor Minnick is a deep and fiery brother that has a passion for the development of Godly men. It was his initial men's conference, "The Mighty Men of Mount Pleasant," I attended that allowed me to peek into his involvement with the men of his church. Pastor Minnick has an approachable disposition and he is a very special person to know.

Reginald Smith – I only know Pastor Reginald Smith as one of our conference speakers. Pastor Smith pastors Union Grace Missionary Baptist Church in Detroit, Michigan. He is one of the MTC speakers that presents from the topic of Christian stewardship with a focus on finances. Pastor Smith demonstrated clear, concise, and simple principles regarding Christian accountability as it relates to God, man, and God's money. Pastor Smith and his church typify the many successes that can be realized when Godly men and women employ Godly principles and practices in their daily financial affairs.

Alvin Hawkins – Pastor Alvin Hawkins is the late Pastor of Liberty Baptist Church – Pontiac, Michigan. Pastor Hawkins was the Pastor under whom I accepted my calling into the gospel ministry. I owe my Bible foundation to the structured teaching that Pastor Hawkins provided. I also owe him dearly for his patient nurturing of my gift during the beginning stages of speaking before a congregation, one that he was responsible to God for.

Billy Allen – Pastor Billy Allen succeeded Pastor Alvin Hawkins as Pastor of Liberty Baptist Church. Pastor Allen was Assistant Pastor under Pastor Hawkins. If I attributed one great quality to Pastor Allen that I benefited the most from, it would be his teaching. He taught me how to study effectively and in context of the scriptures. He was also a great mentor to work with during Pastor Hawkin's leadership during his leadership as Pastor.

Anthony Pettus – Pastor Anthony Pettus Sr. is the Pastor of Greater Progressive Baptist Church in Fort Wayne, Indiana. After being transferred to Fort Wayne, I have been shepherded by Pastor Pettus in a "Watch-Care" capacity. I am so thankful to God that after being uprooted from a "One-of- a-kind" church (Second New Hope Baptist) in Ferndale, Michigan, He transplanted me and my family to a Bible teaching church par excellence.

Eric Burr – Pastor Eric Burr is Pastor of Second New Hope Baptist Church in Ferndale, Michigan. This is my

Pastor. Pastor Burr is well known and well respected in the secular arena as well as the church environment. That says a great deal all by itself. Pastor Burr is one of God's greatest visionaries; he founded the Mountain Top Conference. Pastor Burr believes emphatically that the church will not be all that God intends it to be until the men of God take their rightful place within the church. Thus he ascribed the identity of the men of Second New Hope as "The Chosen Men of Standard." These are "Chosen" men, not "Perfect" men, but I am honored to be connected to them. Pastor Burr is committed to the up-building of God's people and the community. He often reminds us that we are "Second" New Hope, but we are "Second to None."

His commitment is shown through the many initiatives that have been implemented within the church as well as those outside of the church, such as the ODDIS Group, a non-profit organization that provides shelter and direction in life for single moms, the Food bank, Magdalene Andrews Learning center, the Home ownership program, and other enterprises that are in the developmental stage. He has accomplished this in just seven years as Pastor. More than anything, Pastor Burr is a family man with a big heart for his family, his church family and God's people.

Finally, I want to express my appreciation to my wife Janice for her love, encouragement and support during this process. I'm also thankful for my family, immediate and extended for all of their encouragement. Certainly, I must express my utmost thanks and appreciation for all of the editing work of Mr. Ray Glandon and the publishing effort and energy of Mr. Steven Lawrence Hill Sr., and the ASA Publishing staff. In a very professional way all of you have enabled me to share with others what God has shared with me. Basically, all my life I have attempted to do things in which I had no previous experience. Yet, there was always someone in the picture: family, friends and/or angels that made me believe that I could do anything. In all of those successes I now know that they were because of Paul's words in Philippians 4:13. It was never me; it was always God.

Introduction

It could be argued that whenever the words "To be or not to be" are uttered, one would automatically reflect on the work and/or words of Shakespeare in the play, *Hamlet*. The German philosopher, Arthur Schopenhauer, said:

> *The essential purport of the world-famous monologue in "Hamlet" is, in condensed form, that our state is so wretched that complete non-existence would be decidedly preferable to it. There is something in us, however, which tells us that this is not so, that this is not the end of things, that death is not an absolute annihilation.*

Indeed, E. Prosser said that "This soliloquy is a meditation on the central theme of the duties and temptations of a noble mind in an evil world." By that interpretation, it's the moral injunction against suicide that would be ultimately decisive, rather than the "dread of something after death," which only symbolizes the usual fires of Hell.

However, the next five lines (starting with "and thus the native hue of resolution...") no longer refer to *moral judgments*, rather, in a similar way *anything* (not just suicide) can become problematic if dwelt upon.

This (along with Hamlet's indecisiveness and uncertainty of knowledge being major themes throughout the play) inspired many commentators to read the choice between the life of action ("to be") and life of silent acceptance ("not to be") as a primary focus of Hamlet's dilemma.

Regardless of whether the focus is placed on "life vs. death" or "action vs. inaction," the themes tackled by the soliloquy (and by Shakespeare's play in general) led to the character of Danish Prince often getting compared to existentialists after the term was introduced in the twentieth century.

In the Christian walk, there is a correlative challenge. What's considered right and what's considered wrong? Is there ever a time when we can justify wrong-doing? At times, it almost seems like the idea that is taught or implied depicts God as maintaining and managing a scorecard and at the end of the day, or week or life, He tallies up and if you have done more good than bad, He allows you to enter paradise. As plausible as that may seem, there is no truth in it. Right is always right and wrong is always wrong.

Much of this thought process falls into the essence of "legalism." Legalism is the practice of trusting in religious activity rather than trusting in God. It is essentially putting all of our confidence in a practice rather than a person. The danger in this idea is that it will always lead to a love for the practice and not the person. The reason the love for the person is so vital is because, for the Christian, that person is God in Christ. The bible reminds us that our God is a jealous God and He will not share His Glory with anything or anyone.

I discovered years ago in my own spiritual life, the more rules and regulations I applied to myself, the more I failed in keeping them. I remember trying to commit to a regular morning prayer time at a certain time each morning. I decided that I would dedicate 15 minutes a day to it. Time won't allow me to detail all of the challenges that interfered with me maintaining and honoring my commitment. I'm not by any stretch of imagination diminishing the importance of consistent quality prayer time. However, if the focus is on the practice and not the person, every time you miss morning devotion or fail to get 15 minutes in, you will feel like a failure. Satan relishes in this mental stronghold. We must train our minds to cherish the time we spend with God, whatever the amount. God is not controlled or regulated by time; we are. He can accomplish in us in five minutes what we may think would take months. It is the desire to spend time with God that He honors. He will show us the amount of time we need to sacrifice.

Any diligent student of the Word of God will agree that there are times when God *seems* to allow a particular act or behavior, yet in other times hold one accountable for what appears to be the same act. However, as the student digs deeper, he will usually find that God has not changed His position at all. Every passage of scripture must be evaluated in its context. Pastor Jake Gaines always remind us that we must apply the "who, what, when, where and why" principle as we search for understanding if we are to be serious students of the Bible.

Sometimes we may find ourselves placing too much emphasis on what a particular individual is doing while overlooking what God is doing. I do not intend to diminish in any way the importance of what believers do in the Christian walk. However, I do intend to reveal what I believe is a greater emphasis of God and a greater usefulness for God when believers focus more on what God called us "to be." It is from that perspective that I associate this phrase, borrowed from the poetic writing of Shakespeare "To Be or Not To Be." I believe the dilemma associated with "do" versus "be" often weakens the spiritual walk of too many believers. In making that statement, I pray that as you strive for maturity and excellence in Christ, a paradigm shift will occur and you will realize as I have that "to be or not to be" is really the question.

When a believer in Christ begins the Christian walk, often referred to as "a babe in Christ," a lengthy list of do's and don'ts is provided by means of preaching, teaching and personal study. This occurs regardless of age, gender, race, etc. From the beginning of every Christian walk, believers embark upon a process of Christian evaluation based on how successful they are in incorporating or emulating a list of do's and eliminating or eradicating a list of don'ts from their life. This is most often accomplished by focusing on what one does and does not do. This is in stark contrast to focusing on one's "isness." I refer to this "isness" as what one is or is not. Simply put, who they Be. I understand that is not good grammar, but it is good counsel. What one does is not always a true representation of who they are. The same is true for all of us.

When believers are successful in their efforts to "do" what they have been instructed as right, they feel a sense of pride and well-being. When they are less successful, they feel shame, defeat and are quite often uncertain of true conversion. The truth of the matter is that we cannot accomplish this in our own strength. (Phil. 4:13)

If we as believers are following Christ, and if Christ is our example, what does He expect or require of us? This reminds me of the many wristbands that were so popular a short time ago that displayed the message, "What would Jesus do?"

I believe that Christians have a vertical responsibility to God and a horizontal responsibility to mankind. I believe the bible supports the idea that when it comes to what a believer is expected or required to do, it relates to the development of their vertical relationship. There are countless passages of scripture that speak to the things man must "do" to develop his spiritual relationship with God. Conversely, I believe when it comes to the horizontal relationship, or man's responsibility to man, the focus then becomes not as much what man will do but what man will become, or as I will reflect on in this work, what man will "be" or "not be." Ultimately, I believe that is the question. My hope is that after reading this book, you will be able to answer this question as well.

(f)

To Be or Not To Be

Is That The Question?

By Reverend

Gregory L. Williamson

Chapter One

The Purpose To Be

And God blessed them, and God said unto them, Be fruitful, and multiply,

Genesis 1:28

In the book of Genesis, the first book of the Bible, you will find the first words God spoke to man. In verse 28 of the first chapter, the word of God says: *And God blessed them, and God said unto them, Be fruitful, and multiply....* It is here that we find man's purpose given by God. It should not be difficult to conceive and believe that Adam and every other man and woman has a purpose. Not only does every man have a purpose, but that purpose is twofold. There is one common purpose that all of mankind shares and there is a unique or one-of-a-kind purpose that we have individually. I will explain that more in depth later.

Some years ago, Steve Martin and John Candy each starred in a comedy, Planes, Trains and Automobiles. The satire involved the many traveling obstacles they encountered while trying to get home. Man invented airplanes, trains and automobiles with a common purpose and a unique or specific purpose. While all three share the purpose of transportation, they each have their unique method of accomplishing it. Obviously, a car is not intended to travel on train tracks. Trains were not designed to fly. I think you get the point. Because man was made in God's image (creativity, imagination, ingenuity, etc.), he has the ability to produce "things" that have both similarity and specificity in satisfying various needs. Since God equipped man with this ability, certainly God possesses this ability as well, albeit on a much higher (inconceivable to man) level.

Have you ever experienced the perplexity of pondering your purpose in life? Perhaps you may have asked if there were really a significant point to your life. I would venture to say that we have all had that strange encounter with ourselves. However, if you haven't, maybe you have figured out your purpose. If that's not the case, then hopefully this reading experience will provide a smooth transition of understanding the revelation of your purpose.

You may see it as an argument, hypothesis or premise, but I believe one of, if not the greatest, foundational principles of life is that God has a "purpose" for every life. I begin here because as you progress through life, you will see the evidence of God's purpose in the lives of His people.

In every aspect of one's life, there is a purpose in decision and choices. That purpose may not always have the best intentions at heart, yet there still remains an intention for a desired outcome. Even man, with a finite mental capacity, thinks it strange when someone demonstrates actions with seemingly no motive or purpose associated with them. If man, with a limited level of comprehension, connects purpose with actions, why would not an all-powerful, all-knowing and all-existing God create man and not have any purpose attached to him? After all, were we not created/made in His image? The fact is, God not only has a purpose for man, but the purpose is unique.

This chapter deals with purpose and "to be." There are countless nouns and synonyms that help define these words. Just a few are:

> Purpose: reason, point, rationale, function, intention, objective, aim, goal, etc.
>
> Be: exist, be real, remain, be there, and stay.
>
> To be: in the direction of, on the way to, headed for.

I want to convey a point now whose theme will be reflected throughout this book. I believe our being here on earth has a reason; there is a point to it because God's rationale is behind it with functional intentions and objectives that are geared to a particular goal in mind. I believe because we do exist, we must be real and remain on the scene with the integrity that says I will be there; I'm going to stay the course. With that commitment, my life will always "be" in the direction of, on the way to or headed for the greatness that God has called me "To Be."

After God created man and made woman, His first words given to them were "Be Fruitful, and Multiply." These words were an instructional command. They also encompass man's purpose. God never asks anything from us that we are incapable of giving, doing or being. Therefore, man was and still is able to carry out this command. But what does this command really mean and how much does it really entail? The first part of the command was to "be fruitful." On the surface it seems that man was instructed to produce fruit. Secondly, they were told to multiply. This seems to imply reproduction. In some sense, both seem to be the same command. But are they really the same?

In John McArthur's book, *Found: God's Will*, he points out in a very simplistic way that God's purpose for our life is fivefold: to be saved, spirit-filled, sanctified, submissive "to Him," and to suffer "for Him." You may recall that I mentioned earlier, man's purpose is twofold: One being general and the other being specific or unique. Well, this is the general purpose stated by John McArthur. Even though you may not see these qualities in all of the believers you know, these characteristics are vital as one pursues Christian maturity.

The other part of man's purpose involves his specific role. There are some qualities that God has placed in each of us that are unlike those of anybody else. I know this is hard to grasp for some, but it is truth. A cursory study through the scriptures with a focus on various patriots, prophets, judges and kings will reveal some strong similarities and some great differences in their persona. Their objective, or I should say God's objective ultimately, was always the same, but He accomplishes it through people with unique individual qualities.

Man is capable of fulfilling God's command to be fruitful because although those were the first words spoken in the command, that was not the first action in that encounter. The passage says that "and God blessed them" and said be fruitful …. The word, "blessed" here, in the Hebrew, means to fully equip, to endow, so He provided what man needed to be fruitful before commanding him to be. What does fruitful mean? Look at these countless descriptions of fruitful: exuberant, uberous, gleby, good, plenteous, abundant, polyphorous, fecund, liberal, eugenesic, prolific, broody, fertile, fatty, breedy, proliferous, rich, bountiful, fat, teeming, plentiful, productive, teemful, fructuous, and feracious. What it does not mean is barren, unproductive, unfruitful and infertile. That has not changed; fruitful means the same today as it did when God spoke the word in the beginning. The same is true of God's use of the word multiply. He said to be fruitful and multiply. What did He mean by multiply? God obviously would not have expected Adam and Eve to populate the earth by personally giving birth to thousands of children. He could however have commanded them to populate the earth by the continuation of offspring through their offspring. That is really the definition by example of multiply. To multiply is to increase in extent; to extend; to spread. To increase in number; to make more by natural generation or production, or by addition; as, to multiply men, horses or other animals; to become greater in number; to become numerous.

> *When men began to multiply on the face of the earth and daughters were born unto them.*
>
> Gen 6:1

To increase in extent and influence; to spread.

> *The word of God grew and multiplied.*
>
> Acts 12:24

If you think multiplication but utilize the principles of addition, the end result will be addition, not multiplication. An example that might be easier to see is a simple math formula. If we add 2+2+2+2+2 we get 10. If we multiply 2X2X2X2X2 we get 32. The numbers are the same in both examples; only the math principles used are different. There is a significant difference between 10 and 32; over 300% difference. Perhaps one of the greatest calamities in life is the number of Christians that settle for addition in life at the expense of never experiencing the unifying efforts that God produces through multiplication.

So let's put things in perspective and in proper order. God commands fruitfulness and multiplication. This is a reasonable command because He is the one that will bring about both fruitfulness and multiplication.

> John 15:5...I am the vine, ye are the branches: He that abideth in me, and I in him, the same bringeth forth much fruit: for without me ye can do nothing.
>
> I Corinthians 3:6-7 ... I have planted, Apollos watered; but God gave the increase.
>
> So then neither is he that planteth any thing, neither he that watereth; but God that giveth the increase.

When God blessed them (Adam & Eve), He created a connection or relationship that provided access for them to fulfill His command. Because that relationship was severed through disobedience, sin ushered in a process whereby man can still fulfill God's command and accomplish his purpose as well. As I mentioned earlier, God's purpose for our life is fivefold. God provides universally what all mankind needs to be saved, spirit-filled, sanctified, submissive and to endure suffering. In addition to that, He provides individual means and guidance to develop that unique or one-of-a-kind quality that He created in us.

Like Jeremiah, these unique characteristics or qualities were predestined to be even before we were conceived. Everything we need, to be what God has purposed us to be, is in us from the beginning. However, it must be developed. If we look at children in their infancy stage, they all crawl first because they cannot walk. When parents see that stage, they get excited, not alarmed. They don't rush off to the doctor and ask if there are bone or muscle deficiencies. They realize that all of the bone and muscle necessary to walk is already in the child. They understand that there is a process of muscle and bone development that will eventually progress to the level of strength required to stand, walk and maintain balance. God has incorporated this same type of process with our spiritual development.

Our first stage in His purpose is to be saved. God allows situations to come in our lives that should cause us to realize and confess that we are helpless sinners, but if we believe in Him, that Jesus died for our sins and rose from the grave in victory over them, we have salvation. Now that is an enormous step, but it is just the first step. Too many have stopped at this point in their Christian walk and have been tossed to and fro by Satan, often causing them to question their salvation. These types of Christians are easy prey for the schemes and devices of Satan. If this seems to resemble you, I must share this with you. There is a strange false sense of relief that eventually comes, and you sort of feel at peace. You think you have defeated Satan and everything is OK now. However, unless this experience has caused you to draw closer to the Lord as it relates to studying His word and prayer, what has really happened is, Satan now renders you ineffective and he doesn't need to attack you, you will do it to yourself.

That is why it is so important to be filled with the spirit. I remember this idea of being spirit-filled used to scare me. I even thought it not possible in some respects. However, as I continued to investigate and study and observe, I discovered something that helped me tremendously. I was comparing my walk, my growth, my knowledge and level of understanding with other Christians. Now, I will admit, watching and observing is not a bad trait to develop. It behooves every serious Christian to have a good idea whom they are associating with on a personal level.

I have seen too many Christian groupies brought down because their association was with church-goers, not people that were committed to spiritual growth and development. I am not saying that everyone in the confines of the church walls have to be perfect. What I am saying is that as you discover weak areas in your development, you want to incorporate in your personal circle believers that are strong in those areas. In doing that, maybe you can be as much help to them as they can be for you. As we spend time in study and prayer, God will gradually reveal to us our strengths and weaknesses. He will also provide the resources through ministry and other believers (as well as His Holy Spirit) to encourage and strengthen our development.

We see this demonstrated by our Lord in Luke 4 where Jesus was tempted in the wilderness. Jesus was and is Spirit-filled and sanctified. As Satan tried one appeal after another to tempt Jesus, Jesus used scripture, not

His opinion, to fight off Satan. And even after He successfully defeated Satan, the bible says in verse 13 that when the devil had ended all the temptation, he departed from Him for a season. The devil realized that he lost that battle but had planned to return at a later time to try again. If he was foolish enough to plan later attempts against Jesus, do you think he will stop at one failed attempt with us?

The people we associate with should never be taken lightly. Just as God sanctifies us by separating us to Himself, we must do our part by separating ourselves from people and things that operate and function based on worldly principles. As we strive to better understand God's will or purpose for our lives, we must focus on what God requires as it relates to sanctification and what it entails. I Thes.4:3&7 says,

> *For this is the will of God, even your sanctification that ye should abstain from fornication:*
>
> *For God has not called us unto uncleanness, but unto holiness.*

God's desire is that all believers be sanctified. Simply put, sanctification is all about self control, the kind of control that requires the assistance of the Holy Spirit.

If we are to benefit from the power of the Holy Spirit, we must be willing to submit to the leading of the Holy Spirit. One of the greatest challenges many Christians encounter is surrendering their spirit to the leading of the Holy Spirit. I must admit that I have heard countless believers make reference to Jesus being their Lord and Savior. I have also seen many in this same group demonstrate submission to the Savior in their walk. But rarely do they submit to Jesus as both "Lord" and "Savior." "Lord" is not a casual dossal term sometimes used to refer to Jesus. 'Lord' or its Hebrew translation "Adonai" actually means Master. A master has full control over those that are servant to him. Submission, like humility, does not mean thinking less of yourself; it simply means thinking of yourself less while focusing your thoughts more on God. Have you completely surrendered all to Him? Is He really your Lord and Savior? Are you truly submissive to Him?

The last point to be made in discovering God's purpose for your life is, suffering. I must admit, suffering is not an easy task. No matter where you are in your walk, suffering is a challenge, one way or another. We struggle with it on a personal level, and then, when we seem to get somewhat of a handle on it, we often have "friends" that enter the picture and instead of providing support and encouragement, they may cause us to struggle all over again.

You are probably familiar with the story of Job. In the earlier chapters he was struggling. In the middle chapters he seems to get a handle on his suffering. Then, some of his friends, family and servants seem to bring him down again, and in the latter chapters we find him struggling again. Suffering is not easy, but it is part of the package included in God's purpose and calling on our lives.

In Matthew 5:44 Jesus said,

> *But I say unto you, love your enemies, bless them that curse you, do good to them that hate you, and pray for them which despitefully use you, and persecute you.*

Now I must say that suffering is even more difficult and painful when we bring it upon ourselves and it is not for the cause of Christ. That is not the kind of suffering the Bible speaks to.

We find encouragement from the Apostle Peter, who wrote,

> *For it is better if the will of God be so, that ye suffer for well doing, than for evil doing.*
> I Peter 3:17

If we suffer for the cause of Christ, He will comfort us in our suffering and he will not allow us to endure more than we can bear. We must remember the words of Apostle Paul

> *Yea, and all that will live Godly in Christ Jesus shall suffer persecution.* II Tim. 3:12

However, the reward is revealed in Matthew 5:10,

> *Blessed are they which are persecuted for righteousness sake: for there is the kingdom of heaven.*

Now, if we go back to God's command to man, to "be fruitful," it should be easier to understand what He was instructing them to do or "be." As was mentioned earlier, when God blessed them, He equipped them with the comprehensive and creative ability to carryout His command. Man was to utilize these qualities within the parameters of God's instructions and in the likeness and image of their creator. He would be successful in this endeavor through his relationship to and with his Father, God.

At the most basic level of maturity we understand that God equipped man and woman with the ability to come together intimately and become fruitful or reproduce. However, it should be equally comprehensive that two people, even with the greatest of endowment, could not replenish the earth's population with the offspring produced by the two of them only. It is more realistic that a message God is communicating speaks to a continuance of their offspring in the physical sense as well as a continuance of their relationship with their creator through a spiritual connection. In carrying out this process, the earth would become inhabited by an increasing number of people who established and maintained a relationship with God while fulfilling God's purpose for their lives as they constructively exhibit dominion over the land.

This message, in my opinion has not changed. God is still expecting us to "be fruitful," and He expects us to "multiply." Allow me to correlate the idea expressed in the previous paragraph to God's expectations for us today. When God says to us to be fruitful, He is saying that He expects us to produce good results that are beneficial and profitable. He desires that we produce abundant growth both in ourselves and in others. The believer's mindset should be focused on adjectives like abundant, flourishing, worthwhile, successful, abounding, and advantageous. That sounds like an enormous undertaking. However, keep in mind that the Holy Spirit partners with us to bring about God's purpose.

When people accept Christ as their savior from the penalty of sin, they are equipped with the indwelling of the Holy Spirit to enable them to fulfill God's purpose for their life. Do they fully understand what that purpose is immediately? No. Do they fully understand how the Holy Spirit works in their life? No. Is it a secret that God hides from them, playing a hide-and-seek kind of game while the person searches for their purpose? No. As mentioned earlier, the first part of the believers purpose is clearly discerned; it is to be saved, sanctified, spirit-filled, submissive to God and lastly, to suffer for the cause of Christ. This could be the most important process for the newly converted believer to grasp.

Too often, a believer at the beginning stages of their Christian walk is excited, energetic and can't wait to get busy witnessing and sharing with others what God has done for them. There is absolutely nothing wrong with this endeavor. However, there is a process that yields greater success when followed. It is called "preparation." Some of the most devastating setbacks for Christians have come from a lack of preparation when faced with worldly challenges. Preparation is hard work. That's why so many find ways to avoid it.

When a believer lacks preparation, there is only one person that benefits, and that is Satan. He will always attempt to entice you with the idea that you are ready for anything. He is very crafty. Sometimes more mature believers will offer words of encouragement regarding your spiritual development. Satan will instantly attempt to shift your thoughts from "praise the Lord" to "yeah, I did that." I will say again, preparation is vitally important.

Paul stresses this importance in II Timothy 2:15,

> *Study to shew thyself approved unto God, a workman that needeth not to be ashamed, rightly dividing the word of truth.*

Furthermore, Jesus chose twelve followers and spent three years preparing them for the same kind of witnessing work. These twelve men were physically with Jesus during this period. If Jesus deemed it necessary to spend time preparing and training them, it goes without saying that we need to study and prepare ourselves for this work. As Jesus said in the gospel of Mark 1:17,

> *And Jesus said unto them, Come ye after me, and I will make you to become fishers of men.*

The salvation is instant, but the becoming is a process. The process comes about through following. Our following today is based on our faith in Him and our love for Him. We must search the scriptures to discover who our savior is and how much He loved and loves us. That is how we develop a true relationship with Him that is based on truth. Satan can't touch that!

If we follow the process of the purpose that every believer is called, which is to be saved, sanctified, spirit-filled, submissive to God, and to suffer for the cause of Christ, the results will be a stronger and deeper attachment to the work God has called us to. After being saved, the believer must sanctify or separate himself to the lord. The next stage is becoming spirit-filled or filled with the word of God. It becomes not easy but easier to submit to the will of God when you learn the nature of God. When these four areas are embraced, the fifth, suffering for the cause of Christ, is a realistic endeavor.

I use the word "endeavor" because this process is a life-long course of development. Within this development is where one finds their specific or unique God-ordained purpose. Our commitment to the before mentioned process is where we reveal to God our sincerity in being a willing participant in bringing about the fullness of His purpose for our life. Now, as we operate in this capacity, we begin to produce the fruitfulness that He expects and requires. You should be sensing the correlation about now. As we live out this level of fruitfulness, other fruit is being produced. Many times the abundance of our fruitfulness is not known. Our lives touch the lives of people we don't even know or may never know through the interaction of those we meet, those we just cross paths with and those we fellowship with. There are countless numbers of people that these people know and interact with that you may never know. Nevertheless, the earth is being populated or multiplied with multitudes of people that are now being led by the Spirit of God in positive, productive ways that constructively impact the world around us, all because you have been obedient in being fruitful and multiplying.

As I close out this chapter, I hope this illustration that God shared with me provides you as much encouragement as it did me. Recently, my job was transferred to another state. I did not have any relatives there, and I spent the first few months alone before my wife resigned from her job to come. I had a lot of time on my hands after work with very little to occupy it. I had never planted a garden of my own before, but because of the favorable weather conditions of the area, I decided to try it.

After discussing the idea with co-workers that had a great deal of experience with farming, etc., I decided to go for it. One idea that I really liked was starting the vegetable plants in small trays that could be nurtured indoors under controlled conditions rather than risking putting seeds in the garden soil possibly too early and having inclement weather damage my efforts before the seeds had a chance to push through the ground. I must admit that I was very impatient. I looked at the trays everyday with concern; when were they going to break through, were they ever going to break through? This might be a wasted effort. However, to my surprise, this actually worked out very well. After a couple of weeks, I noticed a few sprouts pushing through the dirt. A few days later, I had a few more. After a couple of weeks, all of the seeds had pushed through. Some of them were taller than others, but they were growing none the less. Once they were all at least three inches tall, I began the process of transplanting them to the garden. These small plants now had a better chance of success. As I lifted each one out of its tray section, I discovered something that God used to provide a spiritual learning opportunity. I noticed an unbelievable number of roots had developed from the one planted seed. All the time I had impatiently watched and checked and drew confusing conclusions about their ability to grow, there were countless roots growing below the surface all the time.

If you haven't received my revelation already, God was encouraging me as I am attempting to encourage you: as you go about your Christian journey witnessing, sharing, living, helping, nurturing, teaching, etc., don't get frustrated if you don't see a lot of activity or results on the outside. Pastors preach the word of God to congregations of varying sizes each week. All in attendance with an ear to hear, receive the same information. However, some get it immediately and begin to grow while some get it a little later and their growth is seen a little later. Then there are those that do not get it at all. Yet, many years later something seems to click in them, and they take off like rockets, effectively displaying spiritual growth and maturity.

We must remember that not everyone grows at the same rate or timetable. Just like a tree or a building has to first have a strong foundation to successfully stand, so do Christians. Sometimes after we have planted a spiritual seed, God begins to work on the inside of those individuals. As stated earlier, when we witness to unbelievers, we may not see them when they accept Christ and move forward toward Christian maturity. We must remember growth is not our job anyway. As Apostle Paul stated in I Cor. 3:6, I have "planted," Apollos "watered"; but God gave the increase. We must develop a mindset to thank God for the increase as we continue our work "to be" the "purpose" that He has called us to be.

Chapter Two

The Call To Be

And seeing the multitudes, he went up into a mountain: and when he was set, his disciples came unto him: And he opened his mouth, and taught them, saying,
Matthew 5:1-2

The bible clearly shows that God has a purpose for our lives. He also has a calling on and for our lives. The two are intertwined. One way it could be stated is: God's calling on our lives is in essence God calling us to our purpose. Equally true is a process I spoke of earlier, a twofoldness to our calling. The first aspect of our calling is to be saved and sanctified. Saved by Him and sanctified unto Him. The second part of the call involves the specific qualities that are developed in time and during that developmental process, He prepares us for the specific or unique abilities needed to operate effectively in our calling, or more pointedly, effectiveness in fulfilling the work associated with the call.

These essential qualities are developed through the transformation into a spirit filled disciple. As Apostle Paul says in Romans 12:2, "And be not conformed to this world: but be ye *transformed* by the renewing of your mind, that ye may prove what is that good, and acceptable, and perfect, will of God." I must reinforce the idea again that God is very much concerned and pleased with our commitment to do the right thing but the greater emphasis is always placed on being the right person. I will elaborate more in chapter 5 on this need for transformation. However, to shed more light on God's calling on our lives, I thought it appropriate to utilize the principles Jesus taught His followers in what we refer to as, The Sermon On the Mount, at Matthew 5. These beatitudes, as they are often referred to, are the moral and ethical guidelines that Jesus teaches His audience. I like to think that He was really telling them that these are the attitudes to be. These are the qualities that reflect righteousness. After all, that is what He was explaining to them, the righteous requirement to enter the kingdom.

If we back up a bit, we will find in Matthew 4, the previous chapter, Satan's attempt at trying to derail or distract or destroy Jesus, His credibility and His plan of salvation and conveying the coming Kingdom restoration. Matthew mentions that after successfully defeating Satan, Jesus began to preach the message of repentance because the Kingdom of Heaven was at hand or near. As he moved about preaching from Nazareth and Capernaum and on the Seashores of Galilee, He was making His way to the declaration discourse He would give on the beatitudes. However, He would first call for repentance.

He also preceded that discourse with the calling of His disciples. They would become the physical or earthen instruments that He would use to continue His ministry work after His departure. We can see here that Jesus is fully capable to call men to the work of furthering the gospel. In the book, *"Twelve Ordinary Men."* John MacArthur says this about the selection of the twelve disciples.

> Jesus chose to work through the instrumentality of those few fallible individuals rather than advance His agenda through mob force, military might, personal popularity, or a public relations campaign. From a human perspective, the future of the church and the long-term success of the gospel depended entirely on the faithfulness of that handful of disciples. Nowhere in scripture do we find a "Plan B" if they failed. He was capable then to call men into ministry and He is capable now.

He is still calling men and women today to meaningful work in Kingdom advancement. And the message is still the same: follow Me, and I will make you to become fishers of men. This is probably a great place, if not the best place, to illustrate the various processes involved in

God's calling to discipleship. As with everything that God does and as was mentioned earlier, our usefulness in Kingdom building involves a series of developmental processes. You may have heard the phrase used in other applications that someone or something is or was a work in progress. Well that's also the case with followers of Christ.

There was a time when I thought: well, the disciples were very special men with very special talents and abilities. I thought; there is no way I could ever compare with them. Two issues come into play here. The first one speaks to how often we become discouraged or even quit because we compare ourselves to the wrong example. The second involves our looking at the end result of the disciples and not their beginning or their developmental period. We must remember that while it is almost impossible not to focus on the works of others, it is ultimately Jesus that our focus must revert to when we find ourselves off track. In addition to that, the disciples had flaws and challenges as much as we do.

If we isolate the personalities of each disciple, most, if not all of us, can find our own persona mimicking that of one of the disciples. MacArthur even speaks to that point; the personality types of these men are quite familiar to us all. They are just like us and just like other people we know. Much like Peter, there are some of us that speak too quickly or jump to a conclusion before considering all of the facts and find ourselves occasionally putting our foot in our mouth.

On the other hand, there are some of us that seek out other potential disciples, (as Andrew did) after we have found Christ, and we bring them into the true knowledge of the word. Hopefully, there aren't too many Judas like imposters that we associate with that are hiding deceptive intentions while waiting for an opportunity to betray the faith and lead others astray in the process. As unbelievable and destructive as that might sound, realistically, we know those types are out there.

That being said, the main point I am trying to make here is that I am in agreement with Macarthur. The disciples that Jesus chose collectively possess the same personality types that we do. More simply put, *Jesus, just like God, chooses ordinary people that are willing to submit to the leading and guiding of the Holy Spirit to accomplish extraordinary results.*

If you have been busy working in the advancement of God's earthly kingdom for any length of time, you can certainly look back at various successes and exclaim that the end results were solely the product of God's grace, mercy and power, not our own. In the gospel of Mark, 9:14-29, Jesus pointed out this very fact.

> A large crowd approached Jesus, and after some discussion, one member of the crowd said to Him, Teacher, I brought my son, who is possessed by a spirit that makes him mute. Whenever it seizes him, it throws him down and he foams at the mouth, grinds his teeth and becomes rigid. I asked your disciples to cast it out but they were

unable to do it. He asked Jesus if He was able to do anything. Jesus said to him, if you are able? All things are possible for the one that believes. The father cried out, "I believe; help my unbelief. Jesus said; mute and unclean spirit, I command you, come out of him and never enter him again. The evil spirit shrieked and threw him into terrible convulsions but it came out. Later the disciples asked Jesus why couldn't we cast it out? Jesus responded with these words; "This kind can only come out by fasting and Prayer.

What exactly did He mean? The disciples had been with Jesus for a while now. They had observed Him perform many miracles. They had even performed miracles themselves. The problem was that they never really grasped the fact that it was the power of God that caused these great miracles to take place.

When they saw Jesus perform miracles, they saw Jesus physically bring about a change. When they performed miracles, they saw themselves physically bringing about a change. Jesus pointed out that they were unable to cast out the evil spirit because they were relying on themselves. They had not yet learned to deny themselves because there was still a measure of self-confidence that they possessed. Self confidence is good in its rightful place. However, when involved in kingdom work, it is the power of God that we must ultimately and completely rely and focus on.

In fairness to the Apostles, they did not have the Holy Spirit either as we do today. You may recall Acts 1:7-8 where Luke records:

> *And he said unto them, It is not for you to know the times or the seasons, which the Father hath put in his own power.*
>
> *But ye shall receive power, after that the Holy Ghost is come upon you: and ye shall be witnesses unto me both in Jerusalem, and in all Judea, and in Samaria, and unto the uttermost part of the earth.*

I mentioned earlier a second part of God's calling, the part of the call that involves the development of specific qualities that are produced over time. And during that developmental period, God is working in and around us preparing us for the specific or unique abilities that are going to be needed to operate effectively in that calling. At this point, I need to shed a little more light on this process. Although this is the second part of the calling, this process has developmental stages within it.

In the first part of God's calling, He calls men to salvation. The second part of our calling is to be spirit-filled, to be sanctified, to be submissive and to suffer. The apostle Paul makes this point in I Timothy 2:3-4:

> *For this is good and acceptable in the sight of God our savior; Who will have all men to be saved, and come to the knowledge of the truth.*

Salvation is a quick and straightforward process that comes about by simply believing that Jesus Christ is the Son of God and that He died for our sins and was raised from the grave in victory over sin. Our saturation of the truth (the word of God) is what brings about our fullness of the spirit, and the intimacy with God through our sanctification, our submission or humility and lastly, our ability to endure suffering for the cause of Christ.

When you believe and accept the atoning death of our Lord, you instantly receive salvation. If in your heart you truly accept Christ as savior but never go or grow beyond that point, you still have salvation. What you won't have is a growing relationship that provides the constant assurance that you are saved. John the apostle wrote in I John 5:13,

> *These things have I written unto you that believe on the name of the Son of God; that ye may know that ye have eternal life, and that ye may believe on the name of the Son of God.*

Even in our personal lives, we experience a continuous reassurance of who we are and what we have as we grow and develop in our relationships with our spouses, our immediate family, our church and Christian family. We accomplish this by interaction with one another. This is also what God desires and requires. Zechariah 4:6 reminds us,

> *Not by might, nor by power, but by my spirit, saith the LORD of hosts.*

God calls us because He wants to have a relationship with us. Everything we need to know about God and His purpose for our calling is in His word, the Bible. Without the reassurance that is found only in scripture, you will find yourself questioning, doubting, fearing and eventually uncertain of the decisions you make in life as well as the direction of your life. Being filled with the Spirit is simply being filled with God's word. God's word is spirit. As we immerse ourselves in the word of God we will discover that He has called us to be separated from the world even as we are in the world.

This is not going to be as easy to do as it may sound. There will always be opposition for the one that strives to live an exemplary life for Christ. Jesus said in the gospel of John 15:19,

> *If ye were of the world, the world would love his own: but because ye are not of the world, but I have chosen you out of the world, therefore the world hateth you.*

Sanctification is all about separating ourselves from the world or the world's way of looking at life and separating ourselves unto God by studying, meditating and listening to the Spirit of God as He speaks through His word. This allows His Spirit to fill us, direct us and develop a personal relationship with us. As we continue to grow in this process, our understanding of the sacrifice Christ made for us becomes more precious and intimate.

Continuous growth will help you to realize that while salvation is totally free, (there is nothing we can do to earn it) it is not cheap. It comes with a price. Salvation is free but it will cost you everything that you are. It is at this point that we all should exhibit a level of humility that brings about submission. It is not necessarily an easy acquisition, nor is it unproblematic to maintain.

However, when you consider the fact that no one else was or is qualified to pay the price for sin and even if there were, would they? We don't have to waste any time or effort searching for an answer to that question. There is no one else that could have paid the price and because Christ did, that alone should encourage our submission to Him. When we reach this level of discipleship in our Christian walk, we are equipped to suffer for Him or for the cause of Christ. These are the five stages of the second part of God's calling on your life.

When Jesus called the twelve disciples, you did not see all of these qualities within them initially. Even for them, it was a process of growth. Although these twelve men came from various backgrounds, had vastly differing personalities and occupations, they were still quite ordinary. Peter was very bold, aggressive and outspoken. John, on the otherhand, was quiet. Bartholomew, or Nathaniel as he was sometimes called, was quickly a faithful follower of Christ. Ironically, you find him from time to time with Thomas, who was an outspoken skeptic.

There were differences in their political backgrounds. Matthew, sometimes called Levi, was a former tax collector. A Tax collector was considered one of the most despicable professions. The other Simon was often referred to as the Zealot. Zealots were an outlaw political party that hated Rome to the extreme. James and his brother John; Simon (Peter) and his brother Andrew were fisherman. Phillip was said to have been a fishermen as well, but his personality was more that of a process person; a facts and figures type.

There was the younger James and Judas the son of James (sometimes called Thaddaeus) and Judas Iscariot (the one who betrayed Jesus.) I don't want to go too deep into the specific and detailed individual personalities of these twelve; I mainly wanted to point out that they were all very differing men, and yet, Jesus called these twelve, and any student of the bible knows what He accomplished through them.

Before we leave this thought, let's look at whom Jesus didn't call. He didn't call a single Rabbi. He didn't choose a scribe. He didn't choose a Pharisee. He didn't choose a Sadducee. He didn't choose a Priest. There was no one chosen from the existing religious establishment. This was just one example of how totally corrupt these men and their organizations had become. Instead, He chose men that had not been theologically trained by those destructive hypocrisies.

MacArthur points out that it was a renunciation of all these corrupt men and their organizations which had become totally corrupt. The truth of the matter is that these religious leaders of Judaism constituted the core of those who rejected Jesus. Therefore, it is not strange that when Jesus began the selection of His disciples, he didn't select people from the establishment that were eager to destroy Him; instead, he chose twelve ordinary working-class men.

As I close out this chapter, I want do so with a focus on the call to be as it is revealed in verses 3-13. I have listed them below for your convenience as I provide the following concepts.

³Blessed are the poor in spirit: for theirs is the kingdom of heaven.

All believers are called to be poor in spirit. This does not mean poor spirited and down-trodden. God's call is to humility and awareness that our total sufficiency is to be placed on and with Him. Any reliance apart from this describes what will ultimately result in loss, failure and hopelessness. Their possession is the Kingdom of Heaven.

⁴Blessed are they that mourn: for they shall be comforted.

All believers are called to be mourners. Not mourning for mourning sake. Believers are to mourn over sin, godly sorrow that leads to repentance and salvation. Their possession is the comfort provided from God of forgiveness and salvation.

⁵Blessed are the meek: for they shall inherit the earth.

All believers are to be meek. You may have heard this before, "meekness is weakness," but that is not true. Meekness is not a negative quality because others may define or perceive it to be. It is what God requires and it is supreme self-control empowered by the Holy Spirit for God's purposes. They are promised to inherit the earth.

⁶Blessed are they which do hunger and thirst after righteousness: for they shall be filled.

All believers are to hunger and thirst for righteousness. If you are familiar with the Pharisees and their righteousness; this is the opposite of that. We are to seek God's righteousness rather than establishing our own. This righteous pursuit will satisfy our hunger and thirst for a right relationship with God.

⁷Blessed are the merciful: for they shall obtain mercy.

All believers are to be merciful. We are to show mercy toward others as we would prefer mercy be shown toward us. With man, this is not always true. Nevertheless, we show mercy and are merciful because of God's mercy shown toward us regardless of the lack thereof from mankind. We are to be merciful because God has been and continues to be merciful towards us. The obvious precious possession is God's mercy shown toward us.

⁸Blessed are the pure in heart: for they shall see God.

All believers are to be of a pure heart, pragmatist. Not conniving, deceitful, cunning and the like. Children of God are to be pure and good natured in their thinking and believing. How can the heart (which is desperately wicked) be made pure? Our Lord Jesus said in the gospel of John 15:3,

> Now are ye clean through the word which I have spoken unto you.

It is through the washing of regeneration that we are made clean and pure. Our possession as we develop the pure heart that God requires is twofold. In this life, we see God through the perception of faith, and in the new life to come, we will see Him in the Glory of Heaven.

[9]*Blessed are the peacemakers: for they shall be called the children of God.*

All believers are to be peacemakers. You may say, I don't know of any true peacemakers in the world today. Well, I can tell you one. It is our Lord Jesus Christ. He made peace through the shedding of His blood between and all righteous God and an unrighteous sinner. Because we are justified by faith we have peace with God and should display the actions of peacemakers with man as a result of the peace we have through our Lord Jesus Christ. The prized possession is being true disciples and children of God. Reflect on John 13:35 which says,

> By this shall all men know that ye are my disciples, if ye have love one to another.

¹⁰Blessed are they which are persecuted for righteousness' sake: for theirs is the kingdom of heaven.

¹¹Blessed are ye, when men shall revile you, and persecute you, and shall say all manner of evil against you falsely, for my sake.

All believers will be persecuted and often for righteousness sake or right living or standing. You must hold firm to the fact that even in this, you are still blessed. I Peter 4:12 says,

> Beloved, think it not strange concerning the fiery trial which is to try you, as though some strange thing happened unto you.

Luke says in the sixth chapter and the 22nd verse,

> Blessed are ye, when men shall hate you, and when they shall separate you from their company, and shall reproach you, and cast out your name as evil, for the Son of man's sake.

Lastly, James 5:10-11 says,

> Take, my brethren, the prophets, who have spoken in the name of the Lord, for an example of suffering affliction, and of patience. Behold, we count them happy which endure. Ye have heard of the patience of Job, and have seen the end of the Lord; that the Lord is very pitiful, and of tender mercy.

Whether you see it or not as you go through these trials, you are blessed and your greatest possession is the promised inheritance of the Kingdom of Heaven.

^{12}Rejoice, and be exceeding glad: for great is your reward in heaven: for so persecuted they the prophets which were before you.

^{13}Ye are the salt of the earth: but if the salt have lost his savour, wherewith shall it be salted? it is thenceforth good for nothing, but to be cast out, and to be trodden under foot of men.

The common link in verses 3 – 11 is the first two words, "Blessed are." The word blessed is translated Hilariously Happy, Fortunate, Blissful, etc. The conditions during these writings were quite challenging. These people were experiencing oppression that had been going on for over 400 years. Unlike the period 400 years earlier, there was no prophetic word being spoken. The Priests, Pharisees, Sadducees, Scribes and any other religious institutions were providing more oppression instead of relief. Yet, when Jesus comes on the scene, this is the message He delivers. The same message He is delivering to us. And after hearing these words spoken in verses 3 through 11, He says in verse 12 above, Rejoice, and be exceeding glad: for great is your reward in heaven: for so persecuted they the prophets which were before you. He follows that with Ye are the salt of the earth: but if the salt have lost his savour, wherewith shall it be salted? It is thenceforth good for nothing, but to be cast out, and to be trodden under foot of men.

Jesus is saying to us, just as I called twelve ordinary men to an extraordinary endeavor, I am calling ordinary men and women today to continue that same Kingdom work. Jesus used two nouns to describe the characteristic of kingdom builders: "Salt" and "Light." Do you not find it interesting that both words carry the meaning of expellants? Salt, through its preserving quality, expels contaminants. Light, through its illuminating quality, expels darkness. Isn't it amazing how just a little bit of salt can completely change the flavor of our foods? Isn't it amazing how just the flicker of a match can illuminate an entire room.

As amazing as it may seem, it is not a coincidence. We can have this same type of impact on lives if we operate within our calling and utilize the enormous life changing power and qualities that God wants to impart into our spirits. Now, I know you are excited, pumped up and ready to go out and change lives. We must remember "Preparation" comes before Acceleration." The first call is not to do what the beatitudes state. It is a larger challenge to be the person the beatitudes portray. It's not about trying to be perfect and/or flawless. The beatitudes are all about a pursuit to be in such an intimate relationship with God that the transformation of being what he has called you to be, becomes your agenda as much as it is His. No, it is not easy, but it is very achievable with the help of the Holy Spirit. This is the "Call to BE."

Chapter Three

The Place To Be

And the LORD called Samuel again the third time. And he arose and went to Eli, and said, Here am I; for thou didst call me. And Eli perceived that the LORD had called the child.

Therefore Eli said unto Samuel, Go, lie down: and it shall be, if he call thee, that thou shalt say, Speak, LORD; for thy servant heareth. So Samuel went and lay down in his place.

I Samuel 2:8-9

A noun is defined as a "person, place or thing." The word "place" is usually understood to mean or make reference to a location or a specific spot, such as longitude or latitude on a map or an address associated with a global positioning satellite (GPS) point of reference.

The bible uses the word "place" in countless passages throughout the scriptures in both the old and new testaments. When the word "place" is used in the bible, however, it does not always mean or make reference to a location. Sometimes it is used to denote one's position.

If a math instructor were to say, "Put these numbers in their proper place," he would not be instructing his students to put the numbers in a particular spot or location just for the sake of order. He would be instructing them to put the numbers in the correct position so that the correct answer would or could be realized after applying the math formula.

From elementary education even to the present, math remains a favorite of mine. One day we were given several numbers to add together. Some of them were a single digit (4), some were two digits (24) and some were three digits (134). Those of us that aligned our numbers from the right to left came up with the correct answer. Those that failed to put their numbers in the right place or right position came up with the wrong answer.

Often times you will hear the results of a race stated in these terms: first place, second place and third place. All of the runners were on the same track and crossed the same finish line, but they did so in different positions.

Many years ago, I visited a psychologist to seek help with a troubling and painful situation. I knew there was nothing I could do to reverse what had occurred, but it was still hard to deal with. We had a lot of discussion over several visits, but the one statement he made that I remember most was, "You are going to have to find the proper place to put this situation and move on with your life." Obviously he was not saying that there was some physical place that I needed to discover and after placing this problem there, all my troubles would be over.

He was referring to a position or place (which I later discovered it to be in God's hands) that I needed to find within myself that would ultimately enable me to let it go and move on with life. If you think about it, you probably have some examples of your own that fit in rather nicely with this idea. These examples along with yours are proof that sometimes the word "place" means a location and sometimes it means a position.

I thought it beneficial to have this dialogue prior to delving into this chapter. Chapter three deals with the "place to be." Without this prior discussion, many minds might have focused totally on location when I speak of place. There are far too many believers that have stymied their growth and development because someone led them to believe there were shortcuts on the road to Christian maturity.

Speaking for myself, I recall a few. Resist the devil and he will flee from you. I wasn't told about the prerequisite of submitting myself unto God. I can do all things through Christ. I wasn't told that Paul was speaking more to endurance and God's will than he was accomplishing things that were most of the time selfish desires anyway.

When you are in church, everything will work out and your life will turn around. I wasn't told that. *It's not just about me being in church, but church has to be in me.* And the church in me would only come about through involvement with and commitment to God's people and God's word.

As alarming as this statement might be for some, there is no physical place (deacon board, choir stand, particular church pew, particular parking spot, etc) within your church situation or your general spiritual walk that will "place" you in a unique position where God can use you to accomplish great things for the kingdom. It is all about relationship. Your relationship with God has more to do with your position in Him than anything physical. When the word "place" is used in scripture and it is not in reference to a physical location, it is most often speaking to position and/or relationship.

When God said to Moses in Exodus 3:5 …

> *Draw not nigh hither: put off thy shoes from off thy feet, for the place whereon thou standest is holy ground.*

and in Acts 7:33 where Luke documented this same encounter;

> *Then said the Lord to him, Put off thy shoes from thy feet: for the place where thou standest is holy ground,*

God was not saying that this particular spot where Moses stood was Holy because he was standing there. It was Holy because Moses was in a place or position that God declared Holy. Now I believe everyone would love to have a place or a particular piece of real estate that they could stand on or operate from and receive some sort of confirmation from God that it was holy ground. That, however, is not what God was conveying to Moses. As we have discussed in the two previous chapters, God has a purpose and a calling on all our lives.

When we realize it and submit ourselves to God, it is at that point or place or that position that becomes a Holy Ground. It is a place of sanctification that sets us apart for God's special purpose. If you are a believer and know what God's purpose is for your life, you can probably recall the place and time when you were awakened to the fact that you had just experienced the most humbling encounter with the most Holy God. This is without a doubt the most awesome place to be.

The scriptural text that this chapter focuses on is I Samuel 2. This story deals with several characters: Eli and his two sons, Hophni and Phinehas, Elkanah and his two wives, Peninnah and Hannah, and the child, Samuel. These characters all find themselves in very interesting places or positions.

Eli, whose name means Jehovah is High, was in the place or position of High Priest in Israel. Herbert Lockyer in his book, *All the Men of the Bible,* states that Eli was a good man whose life was pure. He loved and delighted in

God's service but came up short in one area; he did not use proper judgment when it came to his sons. Here we have a man in the right place being used by God for great work in the office of High Priest. Nevertheless, knowing that his sons were not living righteously and that they were taking advantage of the women that came to the temple, he gave nothing more than weak warning to them regarding their shameful ways. These warnings were far short of the rebuke their conduct warranted.

Hophni and Phinehas, whose names mean strong and face of trust respectfully, were priests under the tutelage of Eli. All through scripture, you hear their names mentioned with each other. They were partners in evil practices and brought the pronouncement of two curses upon their necks. They were claiming and appropriating more than their due of the sacrifices as a priest, and they also exhibited immoral actions in the tabernacle.

Serving in the place or position under Eli afforded them the opportunity to demonstrate honorable conduct. Instead they failed miserably. They disgraced the priestly office and were both slain eventually in the battle of Aphek where they also lost the ark. This led to, if not caused, the death of Eli.

Elkanah, the husband of both Peninnah and Hannah was a godly descendant of Levi and therefore also from the tribe of Levi. These three are securely placed in precarious positions where tough choices will eventually become necessary. The consequences of their choices will prove to be vitally important. Elkanah has two wives.

One wife, Peninnah, who has children by him, and another wife, Hannah, who cannot bear children. Peninnah, although she has children with Elkanah, is quite discontent with the affection that Elkanah shows toward Hannah. I trust that no one reading through this story finds themselves in this type of awkward predicament. If you read the entire book of I Samuel, you will see over and over the consequences of good and bad, right and wrong or Godly and ungodly decision making.

So here we have several people involved in this precarious situation, yet each one displays their own reaction to it. As I begin to draw attention to the drama and actions of all parties involved, I want to call your attention to the similarities of our own predicaments in our lives. There are usually many people involved in our challenges, and in most cases, each with their own opinions, behaviors and conclusions. The right or wrong choices or behaviors are available to all involved. The righteousness of God is available to everyone. The question becomes: what position or place do we find ourselves in?

I want to draw your attention to Hannah and the place or position she chose. Hannah assuredly struggles with the greater pressure and stress of all of them. Yet, consider her behavior illustrated in the passages of scripture recorded in 1 Samuel 1:9-12 &17-18 and 1 Samuel 2:1-2

So Hannah rose up after they had eaten in Shiloh, and after they had drunk. Now Eli the priest sat upon a seat by a post of the temple of the LORD.

And she was in bitterness of soul, and prayed unto the LORD, and wept sore.

And she vowed a vow, and said, O LORD of hosts, if thou wilt indeed look on the affliction of thine handmaid, and remember me, and not forget thine handmaid, but wilt give unto thine handmaid a man child, then I will give him unto the LORD all the days of his life, and there shall no razor come upon his head.

And it came to pass, as she continued praying before the LORD, that Eli marked her mouth.

Then Eli answered and said, Go in peace: and the God of Israel grant thee thy petition that thou hast asked of him.

And she said, Let thine handmaid find grace in thy sight. So the woman went her way, and did eat, and her countenance was no more sad.

1 Samuel 2

And Hannah prayed, and said, My heart rejoiceth in the LORD, mine horn is exalted in the LORD: my mouth is enlarged over mine enemies; because I rejoice in thy salvation.

> *There is none holy as the LORD: for there is none beside thee: neither is there any rock like our God.*

This is just one story coming out of the book of First Samuel. There are many more throughout the bible, unique in their own way but in the end depicting the same overall message: people faced with choices and decisions. Some of the stories revealed people that made bad, wrong or ungodly choices (Adam and Eve in the garden, David with Bathsheba, Abraham and Lot, Apostle Paul before conversion, Judas and others). There were those that showed great character in the decisions they made such as; Job, Noah, Hosea, Daniel, the Three Hebrew Boys, and most importantly, Jesus. The good news is that our Almighty God will bring about His desired end even when we make bad, wrong, unproductive or even ungodly choices.

Now Hannah could have thought, how can I get back at Peninnah for all of the harsh treatment she has shown my way? She could have retaliated by displaying anger and bitter behavior towards her husband Elkanah. She could have developed a mean and hatred spirit towards God. She could have ignored Eli and the Priestly position he held because of his allowance of wrong-doing by his sons. Simply put, she could have allowed depression and/or bitterness to get the best of her and just wallow in self-pity. I wonder if any of those choices would have been yours. In all honesty, I can remember times in my life when any one of them or a combination of them could have been my lot. The fact that these were not my choices were not because of my righteousness. It was solely because of God's Mercy and Grace that I didn't become vindictive and reactive and revengeful.

When we recount the actions of Hannah in the verses above, we are left to believe that somehow Hannah realized that God's purpose for all of His creation (including mankind) is to bring glory to Himself. It was common knowledge that the Spirit of God was not speaking and had not for some time. In the third chapter of 1 Samuel verse one the word of God says,

> *And the child Samuel ministered unto the LORD before Eli. And the word of the LORD was precious in those days; there was no open vision.*

I think Hannah was not only aware of that but was also troubled by that and the open wickedness and wrongness on display at and during the worshiping and the sacrificing at the Temple. I believe this led Hannah to vow to God that if you give me a man-child (dedicated for your purpose), I will give him back to you. I have used that prayer model before, and I am convinced that it gets God's attention and yields results.

In addition to that, if we request from Him the thing or things that will also be used to bring glory to Him, He is more inclined to grant it. She may have known relationally what we read in the gospel of Matthew 6:33,

> *But seek ye first the kingdom of God, and his righteousness; and all these things shall be added unto you.*

Wherever life has us physically, we must be quick to remember that it is our spiritual place or position that will turn around for good all of our affairs, desires, dealings and encounters in life. All too often we don't know why God allows certain situations and circumstances to befall us, but we do know that Paul says in Romans 8:28,

> *And we know that all things work together for good to them that love God, to them who are the called according to his purpose.*

May we also find continuous comfort in the words Paul recorded in verse 31,

> *What shall we then say to these things? If God be for us, who can be against us?*

The place you find yourself right now may not be the most desirable place in your mind, it may not be as comfortable as you would like, but you can be sure that God is fully aware of and concerned with your position at every step of your journey. He will continue to provide the necessary grace to endure your battle, and as difficult as it may be to see it right now, for you, "This Is the Place To Be."

Chapter Four

The Decision To Be

And if it seem evil unto you to serve the LORD, choose you this day whom ye will serve; whether the gods which your fathers served that were on the other side of the flood, or the gods of the Amorites, in whose land ye dwell: but as for me and my house, we will serve the LORD.

Joshua 24:15

Therefore if any man be in Christ, he is a new creature: old things are passed away; behold, all things are become new.

II Corinthians 5:17

Staying on course with the assurance that God has a plan for our lives, we now introduce another aspect of identifying what God's plan is for your life. Our focus with this chapter is in an area that is uncomfortable for most people. It is in decision-making. I'm sure all of us have experienced times when a decision needed to be made but was not. There are consequences associated with both decision-making and the lack or absence of decision-making. It goes without saying, good decisions usually yields good results, but poor decisions and no decision at all will almost always lead to poor results and sometimes, devastation.

Joshua 24:15 is one of the passages in scripture that I will be using to convey the importance, necessity, detail and criticality of not only decision-making but proper decision –making as it relates to God and His purposes. II Corinthians 5:17 will also be explored to provide support for the ideas presented on the concept of "The Decision to Be." Making a decision or choosing a decision may be more commonly understood but I want to explore the idea of "being" in alignment with the decisions we make. A sneaky person will make sneaky decisions. A greedy person will make greedy decisions. An impatient person will make hasty decisions. A person of quality will make quality decisions. A meticulous person will make detailed decisions. Now I know that things happen out of character on occasion, but overall, decisions are pretty consistent with the character of the person making them: foolish people generally make foolish decisions and wise people usually make wise decisions.

How does a person become the person they portray themselves to be? I mean, has a greedy person at 45 years of age been greedy all his life, or did something happen to make him that way? Was a selfish wife a selfish little girl as well? Was Job as patient as a little boy as he showed himself to be when he was being challenged by Satan? Was Solomon a wise person even in his youth? Well, I can't factually answer any of those questions. However, I do know that we all develop into the people we become.

When I was very young, maybe 4-6 years old, I can remember something my parents did consistently; they instructed (no they made) us to say thank you, please and excuse me as each was appropriate within their proper setting. We grew up in a church environment and most of our friends were from church or at least some church. Ironically, I recall all of the parents that we were around requiring these same practices. I had 7 siblings, three older and four younger.

Not everybody may have fully understood why we were required to do it, but we did it. Did we mean it when we said it? I believe so. Did the requiring of those behaviors from our parents cause us to be respectful, courteous and appreciative? Maybe it did.

When I look at the lives and behaviors of my siblings today, some 50 years later, I still see appreciation, respect and courtesy shown toward others, and my parents are no longer around to mandate it. Notwithstanding, I have seen later in life, some of the friends that we had then, and their behaviors are far from the conduct we were raised with. Does the requirement of these practices have a direct impact on behavior or do these opposing behaviors simply occur by chance?

If it is true that we make decisions based on who we are, and who we are is based on our environment and how we react to it, and our reaction to it impacts our development, then it must be true that everybody in the same situation will not respond the same way. We can all agree on that. So what makes one person respond one way and another person a different way? I believe it is the Spirit of God, His purpose for each life and the person's response to His influence.

Joshua 24:15 begins with the word "and." Again, that implies that there is something of importance that occurred prior to verse 15. We won't go through all of the chapters in the book of Joshua prior to chapter 24, but if you take a look back after the death of Moses and the installation of Joshua to lead the nation of Israel, over and over you will see examples where God blessed Israel with victory after victory over its enemies. Now, in light of those countless blessings and victories, Joshua has a heart-to-heart discussion with them.

Jehovah God had protected them in Egypt, given them favor in Egypt, delivered them from Egypt, brought them through and across the Red sea on dry land, defeated and destroyed their enemies throughout their journey through the wilderness, provided food and sustenance for them, and now brought them into Canaan, as He promised. Now Joshua asks the all important question;

> *And if it seem evil unto you to serve the LORD, choose you this day whom ye will serve; whether the gods which your fathers served that were on the other side of the flood, or the gods of the Amorites, in whose land ye dwell: but as for me and my house, we will serve the LORD.*

Before they responded, Joshua let them know where he stood; *but as for me and my house, we will serve the LORD.* If you recall, back when Moses was their leader and they were wandering through the wilderness, Moses sent out twelve men to assess the land of Canaan and to bring back a report. Joshua and Caleb were two of the twelve. They visually saw the same things in the land that the other ten saw, yet they brought back a different report.

As a result of the negative report from the ten and God's displeasure with their unwillingness to trust what He said, they wandered in the wilderness until those ten men and all of their descendants at and over the age of accountability were killed off in the wilderness, and they were not allowed to enter into the promised land. What did Joshua and Caleb see that the others didn't? Nothing! It was not about what they saw; it was all about trusting in Jehovah God and what He promised. It was then and still is today all about God's ability to do what He says He will do; not what it looks like we can do. Joshua and Caleb brought a different report because they based their decision on the power and promises of God. It's all about the relationship one has with God.

There are two points I want to focus on here. First of all, Joshua had reason to believe that the children of Israel would again fall back into the same sinful practices that they had exhibited in the past. Therefore, he was not asking them to make a decision regarding what they would do. He was asking them to make a decision regarding who they would choose to "be" in light of who God had shown Himself to be.

Would they develop a relationship with God in light of who He had shown Himself to be and make their decision based on that, or would they continue to function as many people do today and base their decision on what God does for them on a day-by-day or step-by-step basis? Too often our attitudes and behavior are based on what God is doing right now, or at best, "what have you done for me lately." If things are good, we will serve Him. When things are not so good or not what we want them to be, then we complain and choose to operate as the world does. This external approach will never work with God because He desires an internal relationship with us.

Secondly, Joshua not only made his position known, he spoke for himself and everyone within his household. I can kind of hear Joshua saying, if you are living under my roof, you will follow my rules and honor my decisions. I remember growing up in a big family (two parents and eight children), and it seems like there were always more people in the house than just us. There were relatives from other states that came to Michigan seeking employment. Our home was one place that took them in until they could get on their feet. We also had many friends that would spend a night on weekends. Either way, if you were in our home and stayed overnight on a Saturday, you were going to church Sunday morning-end of discussion.

This requirement produced a win-win situation. Most of the time they eventually developed an interest in God if they didn't have a relationship prior and later accepted Christ as Savior. The relatives that decided they wanted no part of that regiment didn't stay with us long. They rather quickly found a place of their own or went back to their home state. I thank God that I had parents that not only sought to establish a relationship with God but provided the opportunity for everyone else within their household to do the same. We all grew up in a church environment, accepted Christ as Savior in our youth and continue to be a part of the Body of Christ today.

God has a purpose for all of our lives, and at some point we will have to make a decision to "be" in Christ or yield our lives to Satan and his destructive devices. My parents provided an environment that exposed us to the character of God and the benefits of developing a relationship with Him. That's not to say that we didn't have our defiant periods where our behavior was not becoming to that of a Christian, but the foundation was established and as Proverbs 22:6 says,

> Train up a child in the way he should go: and when he is old, he will not depart from it.

I'm sure we fought and rebelled against doing things the right way just as most children and young adults do. But after we got whatever it was (the devil) out of our system, we came back or was whipped back to the ways of God. This sort of leads us into the second passage of focus for this chapter; II Corinthians 5:17. Paul says,

> *Therefore if any man be in Christ, he is a new creature: old things are passed away; behold, all things are become new.*

I recall reading a story about a real estate agent that was showing an old warehouse building to a prospective buyer. The building had been empty for months and needed repairs. Vandals had damaged the doors, smashed the windows, and trash was spread around throughout the interior. As he showed the prospective buyer the property, he stated that if purchased, prior to the closing, the broken windows and any existing structural damage would be corrected and the garbage would be cleared out as well.

The prospective buyer said to the agent, "You don't have to waste any time or effort with that. My interest is not in what the building used to be or currently is. When I take over this property, I'm going to build something completely different. I don't want the building; I want the site."

Compared with the renovation God has in mind for our new lives, our efforts and attempts to improve ourselves are as inconsequential as sweeping a warehouse scheduled for the wrecking ball. When we become

God's, the old life is over. He makes all things new. All he wants is the site and the permission to build.

Paul begins this passage in II Corinthians with the word "therefore" which means something happened "before" the information given at verse 17. All sixteen verses prior to verse seventeen speaks to the relationship a believer has in Christ. It is that relationship that develops the Christ-like character that encourages other believers and at the same time, infuriates non-believers. It is that relationship that causes the struggle in our comfort or the conflict in our inner man.

Satan revels in his attempts to defeat us by telling us that we are no different after accepting Christ than we were before we were saved. But God says, "If any man "be" in Christ, he is a new creation; old things are passed away; behold, all things are become new." The question is, are you going to believe God, who is unable to lie, or Satan, who is the father of lies and only seeks to kill, steal and destroy?

Satan is shallow and seeks to impress upon us to operate using that same low level mentality. He wants us to focus on the exterior. He knows that before and after our salvation, our outer physical world remains the same. If you were 5 feet 7 inches tall before salvation, you will be 5 feet 7 inches tall after you are saved. If you were working at a bad job before you got saved, you will still have that same job waiting for you after you are saved. The difference, however, is that the inside, the interior, the inner man is now connected to a power source that has put in progress a process that functions in a new way, a more effective way, a more powerful way, a way that aligns itself with the will and purposes of God.

So how is it that we are a new creation? Paul says in our focus scripture, If any man "be" in Christ. That's the first requirement, you must be in Christ. You must be born again (John 3:3) to experience the newness of a kingdom life. The new creation is in contrast to our former position in Adam. In Adam, man was doomed to die and was under hopeless condemnation (Rom 5:11-21). In this respect, the old things are therefore said to be passed away in the sense that the believer in Christ has an entirely new position. The new believer now belongs to the new creation instead of the old; the Second Adam (Christ) instead of the First Adam. We find confirmation at I Corinthians 15:45 –

> *And so it is written, the first man Adam was made a living soul; the last Adam was made a quickening spirit.*

This new life presupposes a newness of heart as well. When the scriptures speak of walking, it is making reference to the course and character of one's life, which must be new. One writer put it this way: Walking by new rules, towards new ends, from new principles. We must now make new choices of direction. Choose new paths to walk in, new leaders to follow and new companions to walk with. Old things should pass away, and all things should become new. Such a person is something he formerly was not and does things he did not. This newness is to be alive to God through Christ, to intimately communicate with God and have a high and

reverent regard for Him. He should not only have a great and committed concern for Him, but he should also delight in Him (Psalms 1:2). This is to be alive to God.
The love of God reigning in the heart is the life of the soul towards God. Christ is our spiritual life; there is no living to God but through Him—through Christ as the Author and Maintainer of this life; through Christ as the Head from whom we receive vital influence; through Christ as the Root by which we derive sap and nourishment, and so live. In living to God, Christ is all in all. *For in him we live, and move, and have our being;* (Acts 17:28a portion).

In verses 18 and 19 of II Corinthians 5 Paul shares these words regarding *reconciliation* –

> *And all things are of God, who hath reconciled us to himself by Jesus Christ, and hath given to us the ministry of reconciliation; To wit, that God was in Christ, reconciling the world unto himself, not imputing their trespasses unto them; and hath committed unto us the word of reconciliation.*

All things done are of God, who reconciled us. God was in Christ reconciling the world unto Him; Him, (Christ), He made to be sin on our behalf. There were and are three agents involved in the process, but God was and is in control of them all. God is the subject, man is the object, and Christ is the means. J. F. Walvoord says in a study on The Person and Work of Christ, because man is given the new standing of being reconciled to God, he also has the ministry of reconciliation. Verse 19 reveals a phrase "to wit," meaning that God was in Christ reconciling the world unto himself, not reckoning unto them their trespasses. Here, God has reconciled man unto himself by the act of imputation. He does not impute their sins to them, but instead imputed sin to Christ.

The appeal is that God has already provided reconciliation for all, but it is effective only when received by the personal faith of the individual. The contrast is between provision and application. The provision is for all. The application is to those who believe. Those who are already reconciled to God are the ambassadors through whom the message is delivered to those who have not yet availed themselves of the mercy of God.

The recipient of the message of reconciliation must receive the reconciliation. Only God and God alone reconciles men to Himself. As we have previously seen, to be reconciled symbolizes an active process of cooperation on man's part. Man cannot achieve reconciliation with God by himself, but he does reserve the individual right to refuse it.

The work of Christ upon the cross is what brought about our reconciliation. Him who knew no sin, God made to be sin on our behalf; that we might become the righteousness of God in him (II Cor. 5:21). It was the act of Christ in becoming sin by the imputation of the sins of the whole world to Him (I John 2:2) that made possible reconciliation of a sinner to God.

Even after satisfying every requirement necessary to redeem man from sin, God continues to work out this newness of life, this new creative work in the believer's life. God does this through the agent of the Holy Spirit who provides the necessary ability and proficiency to perform and develop Christ-like character in the believer. Christ-like behavior is nothing new to Christ. He already demonstrated appropriate behavior to the highest level. Now He wants to demonstrate the same in us. So in reality, He lives the perfect life in us and gives us the credit. The real truth of the matter is that we can do nothing without being in Christ, without being connected to Christ.

Listen to what Jesus says in John 15:4-5.

> *Abide in me, and I in you. As the branch cannot bear fruit of itself, except it abide in the vine; no more can ye, except ye abide in me.*
>
> *I am the vine, ye are the branches: He that abideth in me, and I in him, the same bringeth forth much fruit: for without me ye can do nothing.*

This, however, does not occur overnight. This renewing is a work in progress, but it is a work that will be completed. God does not call men to do something that they cannot do; nor does He call a man and not equip him with what he needs to complete it. The only prerequisite is that the man be in Christ.

Romans 8:30-31 says,

> *Moreover whom he did predestinate, them he also called: and whom he called, them he also justified: and whom he justified, them he also glorified. What shall we then say to these things? If God be for us, who can be against us?*

Every true believer dies in Christ and is raised to new life in Him. And everyone who dies and is raised in Christ is given new life that they might no longer live selfishly for their own benefit, but sacrificially in the service of Christ who gave Himself sacrificially for them. Every Christian is a new creature, and he is what he is *in Christ*. Every Christian was once dead in his or her transgressions and sins, hopeless and helpless apart from the grace of God in Jesus Christ. This is the message Paul conveys at Galatians 2:20 –

> *I am crucified with Christ: nevertheless I live; yet not I, but Christ liveth in me: and the life which I now live in the flesh I live by the faith of the Son of God, who loved me, and gave himself for me.*

Every Christian is saved by his identification with Christ in His death, burial, and resurrection. Thus, every Christian is equal in his or her standing before God. This means we cannot practice discrimination within the body of Christ. We must view Christ differently in the light of His death, burial, and resurrection. And likewise, we must view differently all those who have identified with Christ in His death, burial, and resurrection. We must not look upon them in terms of what they bring to their relationship with Christ but in terms of *what they have become in Him*.

A man's status or accumulation of things contributes nothing to the cross of Christ, nor do they add anything towards their salvation. What a man was before his identification with our Lord's death, burial, and resurrection contributes nothing to his standing before God or men in Christ. When we are joined to Christ by faith, the old creation dies with Christ, and a whole new creation comes into being. What we were before our salvation—no matter how good or great it may appear to men—means nothing in regard to our status in Christ.

In a study titled *"Out with the old, in with the new,"* Bob Deffinbaugh points out that there is absolutely no basis for pride in Christ. What we are in Christ is due solely to His work on our behalf. Whatever we are, whatever we have, or whatever we do as new creations in Christ, it is the result of God's mercy and grace. How dare we attempt to take credit for it as though it were our own doing.

Paul's main focus in this verse speaks to the way we view others who are in Christ. It is totally true that, in Christ, all of our sins are forgiven and forever washed clean through the blood of Jesus Christ. With that being said, it needs to be pointed out that Paul is primarily teaching us here that too many believers place enormous weight on those things we bring with us into the faith, things we wrongly suppose make us superior to some other saints. Now what kind of things might Paul have had in mind? One example might be the pride of the Scribes, Pharisees, false apostles, and many of the Jewish people as a whole. They were proud of their Jewishness, as though this made them superior to Gentiles. Listen to Paul's words from Galatians 2:15 –

> *We who are Jews by nature, and not sinners of the Gentiles.*

Attitudes of superiority can be and often are very destructive, not only to the body of Christ but to the general public as well.

We began this chapter focusing on the "Decision" to "Be." We used two passages from scripture (Joshua 24:15 and II Cor. 5:17) to support this position. Joshua had to make decisions as a follower of Moses and as a leader of the Israelites after the death of Moses. In both responsibilities he was faithful in his duties to Moses and trustworthy in his confidence in God. The decisions he made were righteous not just because of what he said but because the decision he made derived from the integrity of the person he was.

Paul makes a statement under somewhat different circumstances but certainly just as important as what we find Joshua conveying to the Israelites. Paul reveals a plethora of blessings, provisions, protection, and ultimately an unmatched sacrifice that God has made on our behalf in the person of Jesus Christ. In light of this, it seems obvious what a person's response would be. However, in spite of the love, care and provision that God has made and continues to make, many men still make a decision not to believe in Him. I pray your decision is to "BE" in Christ and "BE" a new creation. I pray that your decision is like Joshua's: but as for me and my house, we will serve the Lord. That, my friends, is not just the decision to make; that is "the Decision To Be."

Chapter Five

The Need To Be

And he shall be like a tree planted by the rivers of water, that bringeth forth his fruit in his season; his leaf also shall not wither; and whatsoever he doeth shall prosper.

Psalms 1:3

Now that we have established that God has a purpose, a call, and a place that requires a personal decision for and on our lives, we will now consider the "need" to be. Whether you are reading this book in the 21st century or later, there is a restlessness that mankind wrestled with in time past does, now and will continue to in the future as long as he persists in contriving in a role in which he was never intended to function.

The referenced scripture above for this chapter begins with the word "and." That implies that something was said prior that provides meaning to what's about to be said. The point being referred to is that the "blessed man" meditates in and on the law of the Lord. The law of the Lord is the word of the Lord.

It is the word of God that produces the character in man that is depicted in verse three. And he shall; the man that meditates on God's word is assured by the affirmation of the word used "shall be." The word of God says in Isaiah 55:11,

> *So shall my word be that goeth forth out of my mouth: it shall not return unto me void, but it shall accomplish that which I please, and it shall prosper in the thing whereto I sent it.*

Hebrews 6:17-18 tells us

> *Wherein God, willing more abundantly to shew unto the heirs of promise the immutability of his counsel, confirmed it by an oath: That by two immutable things, in which it was impossible for God to lie, we might have a strong consolation, who have fled for refuge to lay hold upon the hope set before us.*

When God says, "it shall be" or "he shall be," believe me, it shall and will be. There is a confidence level that man or mankind develops as a result of meditating, memorizing, practicing, rehearsing and imitating the behavior of Christ. When man follows these practices, he weakens Satan's ability to entice, deceive, dupe, confuse and ultimately bring about destructive behavior in man. Satan wants to influence man by encouraging a dependence on worldly values and methods. This leads to a loss of character and integrity. When man is led by a faulty character and a lack of integrity, anything goes, and he will destroy himself unless he repents and allow God to re-align his path. Psalms 119:105 tells us,

> *Thy word is a lamp unto my feet, and a light unto my path.*

This does not mean that the "blessed man" won't make mistakes or encounter many of the same challenges of others who don't study and meditate and apply God's word to their lives. What it does mean, however, is that the man that follows Godly instruction will develop a Godly conscience, and when behaviors that oppose or conflicts with his spiritual nature occur, he will repent and turn away from wrong and pursue that which is right. The difference in the two is not based on or determined by what they do but who they are.

The verse goes on to say, and he shall be "like a tree." What is the purpose of a tree? Why does he need to be like a tree? What is the significance of him being like a tree?

There are many comparable facets about trees and their relationship characteristically with that of man. The first being the variety we find in trees. There are trees that provide nourishment, such as fruit trees. There are trees that provide shade. A tree makes oxygen, seizes carbon, restores nitrogen and distills water. Trees provide safe havens for birds and many other creatures. These are just some of the benefits of trees. Your mind is probably already correlating some of the similarities that are shared by trees and man. The most noticeable difference is that trees carryout their purpose instinctively; they have no choice, but that doesn't negate the need for their purpose. The need for man to fulfill his purpose, even as it relates to the similarities of a tree, is equally if not more critical.

Man needs to be like a tree because just as a tree can be of many types and varieties, man needs to know that God has a different purpose for every man. The need is great because there are qualities that trees possess that other forms of plant life cannot fulfill. Flowers and plants are not durable enough. In many instances, they cannot survive inclement weather. Shrubs and other like plant life cannot reach the heights to provide the shade of an Oak or Maple. Trees, properly nourished, develop root systems that provide stability and sustainability. Pine trees don't attempt to produce apples. Willow trees are not expected to produce walnuts. The point being made is that trees are of a certain type, they produce according to that tree type and there is great balance in nature because of it; everything serves its intended purpose. That, my friend is one very important reason why man has a "need to be" like a tree.

In the gospel of John chapter 15 and verses 1-5, Jesus explains to the disciples the importance of relationship and being in your proper place.

I am the true vine, and my Father is the husbandman.

Every branch in me that beareth not fruit he taketh away: and every branch that beareth fruit, he purgeth it, that it may bring forth more fruit.

Now ye are clean through the word which I have spoken unto you.

Abide in me, and I in you. As the branch cannot bear fruit of itself, except it abide in the vine; no more can ye, except ye abide in me.

I am the vine, ye are the branches: He that abideth in me, and I in him, the same bringeth forth much fruit: for without me ye can do nothing.

We are branches and we are not expected to fulfill the responsibilities of the vine or the Husbandman. In fact, we are not even expected to produce. Our responsibility is to maintain our proper relationship so that as the vine produces fruit within the branch, we will bear it. We are expected to be bearers of the fruit that God, through the Holy Spirit, produces within the branch. Too often we create unnecessary problems trying to do things that are out of order.

The significance is enormous. The proclivity to deceive, destroy and demolish runs rampant in our society. If never another person was added to the current number, there would still remain far too many destructive tendencies, desires and intentions. There are many agents of Satan fully functional and operational looking for every opportunity available to them to "still, kill and destroy." This depraved conduct alone evokes a need for Christian men to be what God has purposed them to be, and in this instance it's "like a tree."

Just like trees that provide nourishment to sustain life and satisfy appetites, man should exhibit the same. Just like all trees stretching and reaching upward as though they can reach the sky. Just as some trees provide shade from intolerable heat, man needs to have an attitude, desire and commitment to provide a cool place for those around them that are experiencing the pressures of over-heating. The best remedy for excessive sunlight is excessive light from the Son. I'm talking about Jesus, the light of the world.

Too many people are experiencing heat overload in areas like failed mortgages, student loans, unemployment, divorce, loss of loved ones, wayward children, drug abuse, domestic violence, alcoholism, etc. The blessed man may not be able to resolve these issues, but he can provide some spiritual encouragement, direction, support, advice, help, SHADE!

Just as trees produce oxygen, nitrogen and other needed elements in the atmosphere, man should contribute to the air quality in their environment. When man inhales, he takes in air. When he exhales, he releases air. However, the air taken in does not come out the same as it went in. The composition of exhaled air is very different from the composition of inhaled air. Inhaled air has the same composition as normal air, it contains:

- 78% nitrogen

- 21% oxygen
- 1% inert gas such as argon
- 0.04% carbon dioxide
- little water vapor

Exhaled air contains less oxygen and more carbon dioxide; it is also saturated with water vapor. Exhaled air contains:

- 78% nitrogen
- 17% oxygen
- 1% inert gas such as argon
- 4% carbon dioxide
- saturated with water vapor

The difference between the amount of oxygen in inhaled and exhaled air is equal to the difference in the amount of carbon dioxide in exhaled and inhaled air. I don't want to get too involved in the chemistry aspects of breathing. I just think it's important to point out that our bodies were designed by God to perform life sustaining functions that can sometimes go unnoticed or are just unknown. Psalms 139:14 tells us

> *We are fearfully and wonderfully made: marvelous are thy works; and that my soul knoweth right well.*

And he begins that passage by exclaiming I will praise thee. The blessed man ought to always give praise to God for all that He is and all the wondrous things He has done in us and for us. We do indeed need to be like a tree. We should be a breath of fresh air to those we encounter in life.

Just as trees provide a safe haven for birds and such, man needs to provide and be a safe haven for those in need of a great tree, whether it is a need for food, air, shade or stability. The blessed man should always be someone that those in need can come to for needed comfort.

The verse goes on to say "planted by the rivers of waters." First let me say that trees are not planted, seeds are. If a tree is planted, it is transplanted. What the psalmist is saying here is that God transplants trees (man) where his type or purpose is needed. He transplants man where the nourishment necessary to fulfill his purpose is available in abundance. We have no need that God cannot and does not provide for through His Rivers of waters.

Sometimes those rivers might be resources from other believers. Sometimes it may be some form of seclusion that enables man or requires man to rely totally on God for his sustenance. This may be done through a process where man's strength and ability to developed through an earthly support system that is gradually taken away and replaced with a spiritual consciousness that propels him to another level. One example is when man transplants a tree, often times what I call a "prop-stick" is hammered into the ground that provides an anchor. The transplanted tree is then tied to the prop-stick to help support it during high winds, heavy rains, and any other challenge that might interfere with its ability to stand straight and not be pushed or blown over. After a period of time (when a root system strong enough to hold it up and supply the necessary water and nutrients from the ground) the prop-stick is removed. In this stage as the winds and other elements that challenge the trees stamina are encountered, the tree has developed a root base that is strong enough to withstand them, and with each victory over these elements, it becomes a little stronger to withstand even greater challenges in the future.

If the prop-stick is left attached too long, the root system does not develop at the proper rate and eventually becomes dependant on the prop-stick for its survival. If it is never removed, the root system is stunted and never develops the root base to survive on its own. You can see the similarities of the tree and man in this regard.

As God provides help and support for us in the midst of our struggles in life, man is to learn and gain the necessary strength from these experiences so he won't be rocked or thrown off course when similar challenges come later in life. Just like a tree, if the earthly support is relied upon too long or forever, growth is stunted or may not occur at all. This often leads to so many Christians experiencing feelings of defeated lives in their walk. The level of faith that comes from a personal relationship with God is never developed to the point that it should be or needs to be.

The good news is that our God is a God that is not limited by time. He is a God that brings about His purpose for man in seasons. The verse goes on to say that the blessed man will be fruitful in his season. God is not controlled by time, but He does control timing. One thing I learned about gardening: if you get too early of a start in planting vegetables, like planting in the wrong season, the plants will sometimes break through the ground too soon, before the temperatures are warm enough to support them, and they will either die or not grow and produce as they would if the temperature or timing had been more appropriate.

The blessed man will not have this experience. As God orchestrates his season and his timing, he will find himself at the right place, at the right time and with the right resources. Imagine the frustration when a well qualified mechanic shows up on time but has the wrong tools.

I can recall many years where the orange crop in Florida was ruined because the trees budded at the time they usually do every year but then a cold front came through later than usual and ruined the fruit's potential. This year in Indiana, there was more rain in the early season than usual and the corn crop was affected. The latter part of the verse says that even his leaf shall not wither. For the blessed man that focuses on, trusts in and is guided by the word of God, doesn't encounter these issues because God orchestrates the fruit, the leaves, and the season.

This blessed man has established such a relationship with God through His word that God's desires have become his. His heart is bent toward God in all things. He considers and counsels with God before making any and all decisions. Consider the blessed result of this commitment. The last part of this verse says "and whatsoever he does shall prosper." It probably doesn't need to be said, but I will. This portion of verse three is not speaking specifically to financial prosperity, but it includes it. What the writer is saying is that this blessed man only seeks what God desires for him. He seeks it to provide the needed resources to accomplish his God given purpose. He has in fact aligned his will with the will of God.

I want to make these latter comments in reference to this chapter's focus verse. We have looked at several correlative aspects of a tree and man. One aspect we have not discussed is the purpose a tree provides when its useful tree life comes to an end. Whether it is grown on a tree farm for harvesting or it dies due to conditions such as poor soil quality or disease, it still serves a purpose.

Foresters will cut the tree down and either mill it to produce lumber to build flooring and other wood products used for construction purposes or cut it up into small enough pieces to be used for fire wood. I'm sure there are other uses not mentioned as well. However, each of these uses, even after the tree is dead, provides protection, security, shelter, warmth, employment and other supportive characteristics for sustaining quality of life needs for man.

Just like a tree, man needs to live his life in such a way spiritually that even when he dies, others continue to benefit as a result of the way he lived. There is no prosperity greater than this. What would our world be like if there were a great many men and women that lived life according to this verse? In Ecclesiastes 12:1, Solomon penned these words of advice,

> *Remember now thy Creator in the days of thy youth, while the evil days come not, nor the years draw nigh, when thou shalt say; I have no pleasure in them;*

Psychologists believe that during the first two years of life, an infant goes through the first stage of life, which is the stage where basic trust or mistrust is learned, thereby producing either hope or hopelessness. In our adult life, we struggle with two issues: the bad habits and behaviors we developed in our youth or our pre-Christian years and the genetics handed down to us. When we become "like a tree," our youth will see a more Christ-like example lived in our lives, earlier in their lives, and the destructive baggage that they currently deal with will begin to minimize in the developmental years of their offspring. There is, indeed, a need for man to "be" like a tree.

Chapter Six

The Challenge To Be

I beseech you therefore, brethren, by the mercies of God, that ye present your bodies a living sacrifice, holy, acceptable unto God, which is your reasonable service.

And be not conformed to this world: but be ye transformed by the renewing of your mind, that ye may prove what is that good, and acceptable, and perfect, will of God.

Romans 12:1-2

Before we get into the meat of these two verses, I want to share two other translations of these passages: the Message Bible and the Amplified Bible respectfully. The Message Bible says,

> *So here's what I want you to do, God helping you: Take your everyday, ordinary life—your sleeping, eating, going-to-work, and walking-around life—and place it before God as an offering. Embracing what God does for you is the best thing you can do for him.*
>
> *Don't become so well-adjusted to your culture that you fit into it without even thinking. Instead, fix your attention on God. You'll be changed from the inside out. Readily recognize what he wants from you, and quickly respond to it. Unlike the culture around you, always dragging you down to its level of immaturity, God brings the best out of you, develops well-formed maturity in you.*

The Amplified Bible says it this way,

> *I APPEAL to you therefore, brethren, and beg of you in view of [all] the mercies of God, to make a decisive dedication of your bodies [presenting all your members and faculties] as a living sacrifice, holy (devoted, consecrated) and well pleasing to God, which is your reasonable (rational, intelligent) service and spiritual worship.*
>
> *Do not be conformed to this world (this age), fashioned after and adapted to its external,*

> superficial customs], but be transformed (changed) by the [entire] renewal of your mind [by its new ideals and its new attitude], so that you may prove [for yourselves] what is the good and acceptable and perfect will of God, even the thing which is good and acceptable and perfect [in His sight for you].

In all three of these translations; Message, Amplified and KJV, Paul is pleading with us and challenging us to "Place our Lives before God." He supports the rationale based on the prior mercies of God and then supports the process by the transformation of God through the Holy Spirit.

J Vernon McGee in his *Thru The Bible* series records a translation written by Kenneth S. Wuest that I also want to share. He says,

> And stop assuming an outward expression that does not come from within you and is not representative of what you are in your inner being, but is patterned after this age; but change your outward expression to one that comes from within and is representative of your inner being, by the renewing of your mind, resulting in your putting to the test what is the will of God, the good and well-pleasing , and complete will, and having found that it meets specifications, placing

your approval on it (Romans in the *Greek New Testament*, p. 209).

Allright, I think this should provide a good or at least better understanding of these two verses. Let's begin taking a closer look at Paul's instruction in detail. In Romans 12:1, Paul uses the word "beseech" which could also be translated to mean employ, strongly urge or even challenge. If you can accept that, I want to focus on the word "challenge" as we explore the concept of "the challenge to be." This phrase, on the surface, may seem a little challenging grammatically, but as we move further into this chapter, I believe the intended idea and understanding will become apparent.

Paul says I beseech you therefore "brethren," which means he was speaking to fellow believers. Staying in line with that audience, I want to focus on the challenges associated with believers. Believers today are challenged with the same kinds of resistance that believers were at the time Paul was writing this letter: worldly views, worldly practices, worldly standards and worldly opposition.

If all of the challenges believers had to deal with were direct attacks on or against God's word, an in-depth study and understanding of God's word would be all that anyone would need to hold their position apologetically. But Satan is much too crafty and deceiving to begin an attack that would quickly end in defeat. He instead uses political, philosophical, civil, moral, psychological and other like issues to stir up emotional challenges, hoping you never search for an answer from God's word, and many times we do not.

We have all experienced a debate or at least a conversation on various issues like, are you Pro-life or Pro-abortion? Are some people born pre-disposed to homosexuality or is it a learned behavior? Is it right or wrong for Christians to work on Sundays? Is Capital Punishment wright or wrong? Should Christians go to war? Is there one so-called denomination that's right and all of the others are wrong? Does God call women into the ministry? This list could go on and on depending on the environment you're in.

We all have been through challenges that are very similar to the one that may have you stymied right now. It is not until we are made to see what God wants us to see that we get the message or learn the lesson or come to understand just how simple it is to move out of God's way and let go and let God. From the very beginning, there were challenges in the garden of Eden, challenges with Cain, challenges with Noah, challenges with Abraham, challenges with Isaac, Jacob, Esau, Moses and for sure the children of Israel. Let's take a look at some progressive events that took place with the children of Israel.

And the LORD turned a mighty strong west wind, which took away the locusts, and cast them into the Red sea; there remained not one locust in all the coasts of Egypt, Exodus 10:19.

But God led the people about, through the way of the wilderness of the Red sea: and the children of Israel went up harnessed out of the land of Egypt, Exodus 13:18.

Pharaoh's chariots and his host hath he cast into the sea: his chosen captains also are drowned in the Red sea, Exodus 15:4. So Moses brought Israel from the Red sea, and they went out into the wilderness of Shur; and they went three days in the wilderness, and found no water, Exodus 15:22

Here we see illustrated just a few examples of the Mighty hand of God providing and protecting His people. These were not minor, everyday, anybody-can-do type of experiences. Could there be any doubt in terms of God's Agape love for Israel, His mercy and grace in operation and His omnipotent ability to carryout His promises to them? Now let's see what happened as this first sign of trouble appeared.

> And all the children of Israel murmured against Moses and against Aaron: and the whole congregation said unto them, Would God that we

had died in the land of Egypt! Or would God we had died in this wilderness, Number 14:2.

And the LORD'S anger was kindled against Israel, and he made them wander in the wilderness forty years, until all the generation, that had done evil in the sight of the LORD, was consumed, Number 32:13.

We are truly blessed in that God is longsuffering with us and His Mercy and Grace shields us from the type of judgment that Israel experienced. It is obviously not because we are any different today than they were then. Even with the knowledge of Israel's history and the memory of our own victories that God brought us through, we still wrestle with and vacillate between faith, doubt and fear. Then at the point where we are almost ready to give up or give in, the Spirit of God brings to our remembrance past deliverances and we muster up the necessary faith and proceed towards yet another victory.

The truth, however, is that many times what appeared to be unnecessary was really quite necessary to develop the level of faith required to not only get us through, but it also developed the level of faith to keep us after going through.

When we surrender our lives to God, there is nothing coincidental or irrelevant that happens along the journey. We may not always understand what it means at the time but you can be confident that anything and everything that you go through has a meaning and purpose that is associated with developing you into the useful vessel God has called you to be.

When God told Moses to go over and possess the land of Canaan, instead, they decided to send spies out to access their ability to conquer it. This was not what God instructed them to do, but He permitted it. All but Joshua and Caleb came back and said Israel was like grasshoppers compared to the inhabitants of Canaan. Over and over we find Israel fearing the Canaanites, the Midianites, the Jebusites, Amorites, and all of the other "ites." While they were fearing those mosquito bites, they forgot that they were in fact God's "favor-rites."

Even in the New Testament, while Jesus was physically with the twelve disciples, they also had challenges they had to deal with. Their greatest challenge, however, was a limited perspective in terms of their experiences with Christ. Some of their experiences were due to the veiling of God that prevented them from fully understanding. However, some of their challenges came about because their focus was on the wrong person. We must learn, as they eventually did, that our success is entirely predicated on our total reliance on God by the empowering of the Holy Spirit to fulfill and complete His purpose, calling and will for our lives.

Just like the children of Israel, our development often times comes by way of continuous faith recycling. Looking back as Israel wandered through the wilderness, you might recall 40 years of what appeared to be unnecessary travel that took them in circles around and about the land that God had promised them. To some, that might seem like a total waste of time. I use the adjective "appeared" because as I reflect on faith and ministry in our day and time, too many of us are traveling in circles experiencing what seems to be or appears to be unnecessary delay. It is not until we reach our destination that we discover what God was doing. With Israel, those that descended from the ten spies that said Israel could not conquer the land died in the wilderness. With us, many times there are issues, beliefs, attitudes, behaviors, circumstances and sometimes even lives that have to die off before we are ready or prepared for what God has for us.

The "Challenge To Be" is revealed in these first two verses of Romans 12. Paul says I challenge you based on the prior mercies or compassion God has shown toward us in the first eleven chapters in the book of Romans. What mercies? Romans 1:29-32

> *Being filled with all unrighteousness, fornication, wickedness, covetousness, maliciousness; full of envy, murder, debate, deceit, malignity; whisperers,*

> *Backbiters, haters of God, despiteful, proud, boasters, inventors of evil things, disobedient to parents,*
>
> *Without understanding, covenant breakers, without natural affection, implacable, unmerciful:*
>
> *Who knowing the judgment of God, that they which commit such things are worthy of death, not only do the same, but have pleasure in them that do them.*

Romans 3:23
> *For all have sinned, and come short of the glory of God;*

Romans 5:1, 2 & 6
> *Therefore being justified by faith, we have peace with God through our Lord Jesus Christ:*
>
> *By whom also we have access by faith into this grace wherein we stand, and rejoice in hope of the glory of God.*
>
> *For when we were yet without strength, in due time Christ died for the ungodly.*

Romans 6:23

> For the wages of sin is death; but the gift of God is eternal life through Jesus Christ our Lord.

Romans 7:18-21

> For I know that in me (that is, in my flesh,) dwelleth no good thing: for to will is present with me; but how to perform that which is good I find not.
>
> For the good that I would I do not: but the evil which I would not, that I do.
>
> Now if I do that I would not, it is no more I that do it, but sin that dwelleth in me.
>
> I find then a law, that, when I would do good, evil is present with me.

Romans 8:1 & 35-39

> There is therefore now no condemnation to them which are in Christ Jesus, who walk not after the flesh, but after the Spirit.
>
> Who shall separate us from the love of Christ? Shall tribulation, or distress, or persecution, or famine, or nakedness, or peril, or sword?

As it is written, For thy sake we are killed all the day long; we are accounted as sheep for the slaughter.

Nay, in all these things we are more than conquerors through him that loved us.

For I am persuaded, that neither death, nor life, nor angels, nor principalities, nor powers, nor things present, nor things to come,

Nor height, nor depth, nor any other creature, shall be able to separate us from the love of God, which is in Christ Jesus our Lord.

Romans 9:15-16
For he saith to Moses, I will have mercy on whom I will have mercy, and I will have compassion on whom I will have compassion.

So then it is not of him that willeth, nor of him that runneth, but of God that sheweth mercy.

Romans 10:13
For whosoever shall call upon the name of the Lord shall be saved.

Romans 11:5-6

Even so then at this present time also there is a remnant according to the election of grace.

And if by grace, then is it no more of works: otherwise grace is no more grace. But if it be of works, then it is no more grace: otherwise work is no more work.

These are just some of the verses from chapters 1-11 that depict the mercies and grace of our Lord that are bestowed upon us. If we look back over our lives honestly, we will see many occasions where we should have experienced outcomes much more severe that we did. In some instances, we should have been dead. Those are the mercies of God encounters.

Paul is saying, in light of our experiences and the enormous sacrifice that Christ made and continues to make for us, we should separate ourselves unto the Lord, seeking lives of holiness and purity while presenting, offering, basically bringing everything before God in subjection to Him as it relates to our life and the decisions we have to make in life. This, he concludes, is our reasonable or rational service or worship to God, not in payment for it but because of it.

This will surely bring about a challenge from onlookers that operate from a worldly perspective. On occasion you might even encounter other believers that will present challenges. This is primarily because of their immaturity or lack of understanding of God's word and will. That's why the principles explained in the previous chapters are so important. It is ultimately one's relationship with God that keeps them in perfect peace with Him.

Paul goes on to say in verse two that believers are not to conform to the ways and practices of the world, but be transformed by and through the renewing of the mind. We will deal with the mind and its renewing process in chapter 8. I do, however, want to explore these two words, "conform" and "transform." One definition of conforming is yielding to group pressures, the ways of the world. Paul warns against this practice because it requires very little effort. It actually requires no effort in many instances. All you have to do is go along with everybody else. There is no thought required. No decisions to be made. When we conform to the world, it becomes easy to say "everybody else is doing it" because depending on where you are, that may be true. We have to be careful and intentional about our environment. If we surround ourselves with other believers, it doesn't guarantee an optimal outcome, but it increases the likelihood of Godly choices.

Transforming, on the other hand, requires work. It will not just happen. There is no quick and simple formula to make it happen. In fact, you can't even do it. Transformation is to be changed in form, to be metamorphosed. It is the genetic alteration of a cell resulting from the direct incorporation and expression of the transformer. Simply put, this is a change that God specializes in. All that is required on our part is to submit unto Him and allow the process to develop. So many Christians spend so much time (sometimes their entire life) trying to transform themselves by doing or not doing various things, only to discover that it doesn't work. That's why Paul says "BE YE" transformed. Just like "being conformed" to the world only requires acquiescing to the masses, "being transformed" only requires submitting to the word of God. When we do this, He incorporates the spiritual qualities and values that will develop in you and produce the peace of God within you. Over time, His good and perfect will is made clearer and clearer as you become more and more acceptable to His guidance and more understanding of His will.

Before I close this chapter I want to address some questions that I mentioned earlier. They were in reference to positions on Pro-life and Pro-abortion; whether people are born pre-disposed to homosexuality or is it a learned behavior; is it right or wrong for Christians to work on Sundays; is Capital Punishment right or wrong; should Christians go to war; is there one so-called denomination that's right and all of the others are wrong; does God call women into the ministry?

I want to say in respect to these questions and any other question that might fit this list, our challenge should always be directed to and on issues, not people. We must strive to maintain the highest level of respect and compassion for people, even if we disagree with their belief or position. I know that can be a "challenge" at times, but any one of us could be struggling as someone else is, if not for the grace of God in this particular situation.

We must always remember that God is Omniscient, Omnipotent and Omnipresent. He is Jehovah Elohim, the self-sustaining One, the maker and creator of all things and people. He reserves the right to do whatever he chooses, whenever He deems it necessary, however He chooses to bring it about, whoever He chooses to use to bring it to pass. Lastly, whatever He chooses to do is the right thing to do, and although He allows us to question Him, we should never question His Judgment. Unfortunately, there are people in society that seem to find satisfaction in wreaking havoc on others. Although God allows these acts to occur, we should not interpret them to be His desire or His will.

What is more cogent to the Body of Christ is this:

> All Christians should affirm Monotheism; that there is One God who created the world and everything in it including mankind who He enabled to relate to both the creatures as well as to have a relationship with Him and that man is accountable for willfully breaking that relationship.
>
> All Christians should affirm Incarnationalism: that is that this same God that reveals Himself in scripture also revealed Himself humanly in the person of Jesus Christ, who as the Son, revealed the Father and after He died on Calvary, rose from the grave with victory over death and ascended to heaven where He sent the Holy Spirit to restore our relationship with God.
>
> All Christians should affirm Evangelicalism; that through faith in Jesus as our Lord and Savior, we enjoy that restored relationship with God and begin to learn again how to honor God in our day to day relations with others and God's creation.

If we are unfamiliar with a controversial Christian issue arising within our culture, don't reject or condemn the believer; our focus should always be in the issue, not the individual. We have a great deal to learn from both

God's word as well as God's world. God's world includes both people and nature. Where God's word is clear, we must be equally clear in our response or defense. We must strive to make clear to the culture around us that our Christian faith is relevant to the problems and issues of our society even if we don't always have a readily available solution to them. We must show the world that our thoughts and actions are different from the world because we are different from the world. Not any better than and certainly not any worse than, just different. We have taken on that "Challenge" as the Challenge to Be.

Chapter Seven

The Way To Be

Jesus saith unto him, I am the way, the truth, and the life: no man cometh unto the Father, but by me.

John 14:6

As we continue the theme of "to be or not to," chapter seven will address "the way to be." We would all agree that there is a way to "do" a particular thing. There is equally a way to say a particular thing. There is even a way to "see" a particular thing. There is a way to approach just about everything. However, with many things in life, there is only one right way or effective way to do or say or see a thing. When we don't address or approach things in the right "way," it can often result in frustration, confusion and sometimes failure. The best way to prevent or reduce the likelihood of doing, seeing or saying things the wrong way is to follow the instructions.

I've never shared this story with anyone, but it might be an appropriate fit to convey this point. Years ago when I was in high school, I took a home economics class (fancy title for a cooking class). At the end of the semester we had to cook an entrée and a dessert for final grade. I had received an A for my spaghetti earlier in the semester, so I planned to repeat that. For my dessert, I figured I would make my Aunt's famous German Chocolate Cake. I got the recipe from her and purchased all the ingredients, and I was all set for the finals.

I mixed all of the ingredients for the cake, put it in the oven at the correct temperature, and the cake turned out perfect. I then mixed all of the ingredients for the icing. I will never forget; I put the milk in the pot and brought it to a medium temperature. Then I added the sugar, vanilla, coconut and lastly, I cracked three eggs and put them in. If you haven't figured out yet, the eggs poached right before my eyes. I was devastated. I only brought enough to complete the recipe, so I couldn't start over. How did this happen? When I took a closer look, I had only focused on the ingredients, not the instructions; I mixed everything that was required for the icing. What I didn't realize is that there is a particular "WAY" the ingredients have to be mixed together to achieve the results that my aunt obtained. Putting everything in the pot brought all of the products together but not in a harmonious way. Not in a way that brought out the best in them collectively.

When Jesus was nearing the closing stages of His earthly ministry, He engaged in a conversation with His disciples. Knowing what was about to happen and the devastating affect it could have on them, he began a conversation that is recorded at the fourteenth chapter of the gospel of John. Jesus is about to experience the rejection of His own people. He is about to be betrayed by one of His chosen disciples. Judas is in route with a band of men and officers acquired through the Chief Priest and the Pharisees to arrest Him. In the midst of all of this, Jesus finds His disciples asleep as opposed to watching out, while He is off to the side praying to His Father.

All of the time, work and effort put into teaching and explaining why He came, what He had to do, what would happen to Him, that He would be crucified, and on the third day be raised from the grave was now about to be put to the test. These eleven men would be counted on to continue the earthly work that Jesus had prepared them for, but were they ready? Had they understood the true meaning of what they had been taught? Would they be able to unify and stand firm on the powerful principles and practices that Jesus had instilled in them?

Let's take a look at the conversation recorded at John 14:1-6.

> Let not your heart be troubled: ye believe in God, believe also in me. ²In my Father's house are many mansions: if it were not so, I would have told you. I go to prepare a place for you. ³And if I go and prepare a place for you, I will come again, and receive you unto myself; that where I am, there ye may be also. ⁴And whither I go ye know, and the way ye know. ⁵Thomas saith unto him, Lord, we know not whither thou goest; and how can we know the way? ⁶Jesus saith unto him, I am the way, the truth, and the life: no man cometh unto the Father, but by me.

Jesus later says in chapter 17 and verses 25-26,

> O righteous Father, the world hath not known thee: but I have known thee, and these have known that thou hast sent me. ²⁶And I have declared unto them thy name, and will declare it: that the love wherewith thou hast loved me may be in them, and I in them.

Now in chapter 18 let's see what happened.

> When Jesus had spoken these words; he went forth with his disciples over the brook Cedron,

where was a garden, into the which he entered, and his disciples. ²And Judas also, which betrayed him, knew the place: for Jesus ofttimes resorted thither with his disciples.

Judas then, having received a band of men and officers from the chief priests and Pharisees, cometh thither with lanterns and torches and weapons. ⁴Jesus therefore, knowing all things that should come upon him, went forth, and said unto them, Whom seek ye? ⁵They answered him, Jesus of Nazareth. Jesus saith unto them, I am he. And Judas also, which betrayed him, stood with them. ⁶As soon then as he had said unto them, I am he, they went backward, and fell to the ground. ⁷Then asked he them again, Whom seek ye? And they said, Jesus of Nazareth. ⁸Jesus answered, I have told you that I am he: if therefore ye seek me, let these go their way: ⁹That the saying might be fulfilled, which he spake, Of them which thou gavest me have I lost none.

We obviously won't do it here, but if you patiently read the entire gospel of John, you will see the personalities of the disciples and the various behavioral extremes that include both successes and failures during their time spent with Jesus. I speak to this point not to berate or rebuke them. I speak to this point to encourage, inspire and reassure anyone that might be experiencing guilt or some sense of failure because you didn't always find success in similar encounters in your Christian walk. This is why I want to focus on this chapter's topic, "The Way To Be." Jesus said unto Thomas and He is saying to us, I am the way, the truth, and the life: no man cometh unto the Father, but by me.

This statement probably brings about the most controversial challenges ever in religious circles. Non-believers reject it because they believe there are other ways that lead to heaven or the next life as some of them put it. There are followers of other denominations or religions that reject Jesus' statement and are angered by it because they believe all religions, or in some instances, only their religion, regardless of its tenets, can get you to heaven or at least to a position of satisfying God. However, if one's hope and confidence is in the mantle of God's written and spoken word, these positions must be discarded as complete fallacy. Jesus said, I am the way, not I am "a" way. Jesus said I am "the truth," singular, "the" truth means there is no other truth. Jesus said I am the life, again singular; there is no real life in anything outside of Him. Lastly, He says that there is "NO OTHER WAY" to get to the Father except through Him.

We live in a time when so many people, Christians and non-Christians are constantly looking for gimmicks and shortcuts. In the book, *The Church Awakening:* Charles Swindoll explains; the problem with a sinking ship is not the ship in the water but the water in the ship. The problem for Christians is not the Christians in the world but the world in the Christian that constitutes danger. God attracts and directs His people through biblical truth that is taught consistently, preached passionately and lived out authentically. But how do you live out the biblical truth? The word of God gives us the answer, but before I share it, let me share this illustration.

I mentioned earlier in the book that I grew up with four brothers. Three of them were older. We would often play baseball. There are a lot of things involved in baseball. If you are going to be real good at it, you need to be able to pitch the ball, hit the ball, catch the ball, throw the ball and run the bases. It's rare to come across a player that can do all of these well.

Nevertheless, I remember when I would get a hit or make a catch or make any good play, my oldest brother would simply say, "Way to be." That simple statement meant I had done something good in reference to playing the game. He didn't have to say, good hit or nice catch or anything like that, just "Way to be." That same message is conveyed all throughout the bible. It may not always be stated in that exact phrase, but you can hear God saying in essence "way to be."

When Abel brought his offering before God and it was accepted, God was saying to Abel, "way to be." When Joseph ran from Potiphar's wife leaving his coat in her hand, God was saying "way to be." When you succeed in defeating Satan's attempt to destroy or discredit you, God is saying "way to be." If we would place our focus on "being" what God wants us to be, we would see how simple life becomes because He will take care of the "doing" that keeps us on track.

It wasn't Abel's offering "per se" that pleased God, it was his attitude towards giving. It wasn't Joseph's quickness and speed or his willingness to give up his coat that pleased God, it was his commitment to the righteousness of God and his attitude towards sin and adultery. Lastly, it is not about how smart you are or your unique ability to resist Satan that made you successful in keeping him at bay, it is the power of God that brings about a successful result in our encounters with Satan.

James 4:7 does not say "resist the devil and he will flee from you" as so many errantly believe. James 4:7 says "Submit" yourselves unto God, resist the devil, and he will flee from you. Some translations say "Humble" yourselves before God. The point is, when we position ourselves in a submissive role unto God, we resist the devil in the power of God, and He (God) causes the devil to flee.

It's not about a scorecard where you try to do a good thing here and a good thing there and keep adding up your good deeds to see where you are. Followers of Christ submerged themselves in Christ and let Him pave the way. That's the way to be. Let's take a look at the encounter with Cain and Abel recorded in Genesis 4:1-3

> *And in process of time it came to pass, that Cain brought of the fruit of the ground an offering unto the LORD.*
>
> *And Abel, he also brought of the firstlings of his flock and of the fat thereof. And the LORD had respect unto Abel and to his offering:*
>
> *But unto Cain and to his offering he had not respect. And Cain was very wroth, and his countenance fell.*

There was nothing wrong with Cain bringing an offering of fruit. Cain was a gardener and Abel was a shepherd, if you will, over a flock. I have not read anywhere in the bible where a person that raised or produced fruit was condemned. As a matter of fact, good fruit, first fruit and producing fruit are phrases that Jesus spoke quite often and in very positive ways. The problem here with Cain and his offering has more to do with the type of fruit he offered and his attitude in offering it.

First of all, the passage in verse three does not say that Cain brought his first fruit. God wants our first. It does not say that it was his best fruit; just the fruit of the ground. God wants our best. However, take a look at verse 4 …

> *And Abel, he also brought of the firstlings of his flock and of the fat thereof. And the LORD had respect unto Abel and to his offering:*

Now it didn't have to end this way. God said to Cain in verses 6 -7,

> *Why are you wroth? And why is your countenance fallen? If you do well, shall not your offering be accepted? You can still bring an offering; it just has to be the right way. If you don't do it the right way, Satan lies in wait at your door. And he (Satan) will be focused on you to destroy you. And thou shalt rule over him (you have the power and authority to overrule his plan).*

In verse eight we see the heart of Cain and the result after his conversation with God.

> *And Cain talked with Abel his brother; and it came to pass, when they were in the field, that Cain rose up against Abel his brother, and slew him.*

When God told Cain that he had the ability to rule over the devil and his intentions to attack him, He was conveying to Cain that the power to overcome Satan is predicated on man's heart condition. If man submits unto God and his righteous requirements, nothing is impossible and all things become possible. Cain needed to know and so do we, the words spoken to Zerubbabel in Zechariah 4:6 …

> *Then he answered and spake unto me, saying, This is the word of the Lord unto Zerubbabel, saying, Not by might, nor by power, but by my spirit, saith the Lord of hosts. It's not what we do; it's what God does through a willing servant that makes the difference. Oh what a dangerous position we place ourselves in when we misinterpret our position with God based on what we do and not on what we be or simply, who we are "in Christ".*

Proverbs 16:25 says,

> *There is a way that seems right to a man but the end thereof are the ways of death.*

At Micah 6:8, the prophet tells us,

> *He hath shewed thee, O man, what is good; and what doth the LORD require of thee, but to do*

justly, and to love mercy, and to walk humbly with thy God?

Jesus says in John 14:6 that I am not only the way but I am the truth and the life. I can't count the number of times I have heard people, (Christians and Non-Christians) say, "Man, I'm just trying to find a way to make an honest living," and I think that is noble. However, when I really take a close look at what Jesus is saying, this is what I see: honesty is synonymous with truth and living is part of life. The message to me is, if you are searching for an honest and truthful life of living, the only way you can find that is through Me. I am not adding to or changing the word of God, the message is clearly there. God has so meticulously established this that you can't accomplish it through the Holy Spirit and you can't accomplish it through God the Father; it can only be accomplished through Jesus.

As Paul recorded in Colossians 2:9

For in him dwelleth all the fullness of the Godhead bodily.

Paul further states at Philippians 2:10

That at the name of Jesus every knee should bow, of things in heaven, and things in earth, and things under the earth;

Maybe you are thinking; well Jesus can easily say He's the only way; what could He be challenged with? He didn't go through the same kinds of difficulties that we experience. Well, let's take a look at the gospel of Matthew, chapter 4 and verses 1-11.

> *Then was Jesus led up of the Spirit into the wilderness to be tempted of the devil. ²And when he had fasted forty days and forty nights, he was afterward a hungered. ³And when the tempter came to him, he said, If thou be the Son of God, command that these stones be made bread. ⁴But he answered and said, It is written, Man shall not live by bread alone, but by every word that proceedeth out of the mouth of God. ⁵Then the devil taketh him up into the holy city, and setteth him on a pinnacle of the temple, ⁶And saith unto him, If thou be the Son of God, cast thyself down: for it is written, He shall give his angels charge concerning thee: and in their hands they shall bear thee up, lest at any time thou dash thy foot against a stone. ⁷Jesus said unto him, It is written again, Thou shalt not tempt the Lord thy God. ⁸Again, the devil taketh him up into an exceeding high mountain, and sheweth him all the kingdoms of the world, and the glory of them; ⁹And saith unto him, All these things will I give thee, if thou wilt fall down and worship me. ¹⁰Then saith Jesus*

> unto him, Get thee hence, Satan: for it is written, Thou shalt worship the Lord thy God, and him only shalt thou serve. ¹¹Then the devil leaveth him, and, behold, angels came and ministered unto him.

The first thing I want to point out is that this occurred immediately after Jesus was baptized by John the Baptist. The first warning is that Satan doesn't play fair. He knows that after you accept Christ as savior, you are now connected to the greatest power source there is; but he won't wait until you are taught and matured before he comes after you. I will admit that Jesus is a different kind of target, but you see he comes after Him right away. Yes, He is Jesus the Christ, but He is also flesh. Look at verse 2 –

> And when he had fasted forty days and forty nights, he was afterward a hungered.

One thing believers should always remember is that Satan will always come at you when you are weak, and he will always try to entice you with an easier method, route, or simply put, "way." He knows that Jesus is the way, the truth and the life. He knows that no one can or will get to heaven except through Jesus, *but he will always try to deceive you into believing his seemingly insignificant adjustments to the word of God has no effect on its veracity.* That's what he did with Eve, and we all know the consequences of that exchange. Satan wants us to believe that there is always another way. Just as he did with Jesus in the passage here in Matthew, his focus is on the lust of the flesh, lust of the eyes and the pride of life. Jesus is obviously tired, hungry and nearly exhausted just like we get on occasion. But how does He respond to Satan? Jesus used the word of God to defeat Satan and for that reason alone, that's what we should use. Satan said, "If thou be," Jesus said, "It is written." Satan says to us, "If you are a Christian," our response should be, "It is written." In verses 16-17 of Matthew 3, we see these words –

And Jesus, when he was baptized, went up straightway out of the water: and, lo, the heavens were opened unto him, and he saw the Spirit of God descending like a dove, and lighting upon him:

And lo a voice from heaven, saying, This is my beloved Son, in whom I am well pleased.

I submit unto you that when God said "This is my beloved Son, in whom I am well pleased." He was in essence saying to Jesus, that's the "Way to be." And when we stand firmly convinced in our commitment and conviction that Jesus is not "just" the way, the truth and the life; He is the "only" way, the only truth, and His way and truth lead to the only real life. We must tell the lost and remind the saved that at the name of Jesus, every knee shall bow and every tongue shall confess that Jesus is LORD of all.

Before I close out this chapter, I want to share this with you. Living out your God given purpose in the will of God is the most exhilarating experience one can have. Nothing in life will bring about the level of contentment that finding and functioning in your purpose will. I pointed out in the first chapter of this book that God's desire for us is fivefold, to be saved, spirit-filled, sanctified, submissive "to Him" and to suffer "for Him." John MacArthur points out in his book, *Found, God's Will,*" that once you have applied and yielded to these principles, the relationship you will have developed just simplified your search for your purpose and His will. Whatever your passion is, that's your purpose. Could it be any simpler?

Now this does not mean that your walk will be perfect; we all make mistakes and will continue to, but the yielded believer will have a mind that is so connected to the will of God that if you get off course, God will speak to you by means of His Holy Spirit and you will receive it and realign yourself to stay in His will. As we move into chapter 8, I wanted to share this because chapter 8 deals with "The Mind." Your success in this process is entirely based on your mind, how you guard it and whom you yield it to. The following passages should provide encouragement along your journey.

Psalms 84:11

> *For the LORD God is a sun and shield: the LORD will give grace and glory: no good thing will he withhold from them that walk uprightly.*

John 15:7

> *If ye abide in me, and my words abide in you, ye shall ask what ye will, and it shall be done unto you.*

Proverbs 3:5-6

> *Trust in the LORD with all thine heart; and lean not unto thine own understanding.*
>
> *In all thy ways acknowledge him, and he shall direct thy paths.*

Psalms 37:4-5

> *Delight yourself also in the LORD, And He shall give you the desires of your heart.*
>
> *Commit your way to the LORD, Trust also in Him, And He shall bring it to pass.*

I know this may be difficult to receive because Satan has created this mystical perception that there is this deep hidden purpose that God has for you that you will search a lifetime to discover. That's not the way our God operates. God wants us to change the world not by changing others, but by changing ourselves through submission to Him. Again, He will do the changing. I just believe that as we submit ourselves more to the service of the Lord and what He has purposed in our lives we will also hear a soft and peaceful spirit speaking these same words in our ear, servant; "That's The Way To Be" because I am the way, the truth, and the life: no man cometh unto the Father, but by me.

Chapter Eight

The Mind To Be

Let this mind be in you, which was also in Christ Jesus:
Philippians 2:5

In the book of Philippians we find the Apostle Paul writing to the Philippian believers regarding the importance of humility in Christian living. In the *Thru the Bible series*, J. Vernon McGee points out that within the second chapter of this book you will find the mind of Christ; humble, the mind of God; exaltation of Christ, the mind of Paul; the things of Christ, the mind of Timothy; like-minded with Paul and the mind of Epaphroditus; the work of Christ. As we turn our attention to Philippians two, verse 5, our focus will be on "the mind to be." We have now come to the final chapter of this book, and what better place to conclude with but the mind of Jesus Christ. Paul says – Let this mind be in you that was also in Christ Jesus. *Let this mind be*: what exactly is Paul saying?

The word "mind" means reason, intellect and intelligence. It refers to the mental capacity, equipment and qualities. It is the part of the human being that thinks, feels, and wills, yet in contrast to the body that responds to the mind. The mind has reasoning power that distinguishes itself from feeling. It appeals to the intellect rather than emotions. It is also the part of the person that develops alertness and quickness in understanding. The mind is generally accepted as the philosophical center of mental activity and therefore considered intellectually powerful. God designed our minds to have understanding, insight, common sense, prudence, discretion, tact and diplomacy.

In the Greek, this passage says – this is to be the constant thinking in you which also was in Christ Jesus. This exhortation reaches back to the preceding verses (2-4) and connects it to verse 6 which speaks to the "who." The words "let mind be" are the translation of one Greek word which means "to have understanding, to be wise, to direct one's mind to a thing and to seek or strive for." The word seems to always keep in view the direction which thought, in practical terms, take.

For example, it could be said – Be constantly thinking this in yourselves, Be having this mind in you, Reflect in your own minds, the mind of Christ Jesus, or Let the same purpose inspire you as was in Christ Jesus. The epiphany of thought is that the believers at Philippi were being exhorted and urged to emulate or pattern in their own lives the distinctive virtues of the Lord Jesus recorded in verses 2-4. We find there the consistent direction of our Lord's mind with regard to self. Paul shows there the thinking, the attitude of humility and the denying of self, for the benefit of others that should be evident in the believers at Philippi and should be evident in us as well.

The Apostle Paul is actually speaking to the past act of supreme renunciation performed by our Lord in His incarnation and atoning sacrifice on the cross for our sin. Therefore, he says in Greek, this mind be constantly having in you which was also in Christ Jesus. From the KJV bible we read, Let this mind be in you which was also in Christ Jesus.

At this point you may be asking if all of this attention to the mind is really necessary. The answer is a resounding, Yes! If we look back to the beginning chapter of this book, you will be reminded that God has a purpose, a call, a place, a decision, a challenge, a need, a certain way and a certain mind or mind-set for all of us. It is our mind that influences our day-to-day decisions in life. Whether you are a believer or not, there is a constant battle going on all around you, and it's all about controlling your mind. Satan knows just as scientist's do that we are all controlled by our mind functions.

I read an article on-line about mind control. A synopsis of its promise is listed below – "Catapult Yourself to Success, Happiness and Much More:"

> Join us for the Complete Mind Power and Subconscious Mind Power training. Learn how to train your mind and direct the power of your subconscious mind by working with your thought, changing beliefs, and eliminating negative thinking. This Complete Self Improvement System shows you how to achieve your goals by using your subconscious mind power.

No matter what you think about this claim, not only is Satan competing for your mind, he is getting tons of assistance from commercial advertisers, immoral people and institutions, drugs, pornography, an enormous number of various so-called rights movements, errant teaching and, believe it or not, many times, yourself. Every thought and/or belief that is not or has not come under the subjection of God could be working in your life against the very principles for which you stand.

The mind of Christ will see success in a much different way than what the world calls success. The world sees success as gaining power, prestige and possessions. Your level of success is measured against other competitors, such as, how much higher you are than they, or how much more money you have than they do. In the world, assertiveness and aggressiveness are values highly sought, especially in the business world.

I remember years ago when a report came out depicting the amount of bonus one of the "Big Three" CEOs was paid that year. In a very short period of time, another report was in the papers describing the projected bonus for the CEO of the Leading Corporation of the three. The point was simply, we outperformed the other company, so our bonus should be greater. On the surface, that makes sense but should decisions always be made based on factors similar to these? Is it right to make the competition your gage, or should there be a predetermined target? The bible measures success in terms of how much you have given, not acquired and by how much you are willing to serve, not how much you are served.

Every successful follower of Christ must at some point come to understand and accept the fact that they were born to live for Christ. The earlier you come to know this, the better. Every bad, negative, destructive, wrong, misunderstood, etc., event that takes place in our lives, and correct reasoning is not applied or attached to it, it actually works against us. We will blame God for things that happen; we will turn left the next time we have to make a similar decision because a right turn previously didn't bring about the desired results. Obviously, that method doesn't guarantee a good or the right result. The only way to bring about the right result is to make your decision in the mind of Christ. Matthew 6:33 tells us - But seek ye first the kingdom of God, and his righteousness; and all these things shall be added unto you.

The mind of Christ is a mind of humility. Our Lord Jesus Christ existed from the very beginning as the second person of the Godhead. It was He that took the active role in the creation of man and the world around him. John 1:1-3 says

> *In the beginning was the Word, and the Word was with God, and the Word was God. ^{2}The same was in the beginning with God. ^{3}All things were made by him; and without him was not anything made that was made.*

He existed as God and was fully equal with the Father in His essence. Yet, even though He was equal with God the Father, He did not seize it as an opportunity to independently advance His own interests, unlike Satan who could never be equal with God because he was created by God but nevertheless attempted to assert himself above God. Now you may be thinking, the audacity of Satan. Before you let your mind take you too far, you might want to change that, as I do on occasion, the audacity of me! I think we all at some point or another get beside ourselves. We forget that it was God that created us and not we who created Him. I know there are times when we revert to this Godlike concept in our perception that we manipulate into satisfying our wishes, but that's not who God is. That is actually Satan encouraging your mind to think you are being led by the spirit when in essence you are being led by your own spirit.

Paul tells in Romans 12:2 that our minds need continuous renewing –

> *And be not conformed to this world: but be ye transformed by the renewing of your mind, that ye may prove what is that good, and acceptable, and perfect, will of God.*

If you recall in chapter one, we discussed the instant action of salvation if you are sincere in admitting your position, confessing your status and accepting the atoning sacrifice of Jesus Christ for your sin. We followed that with the process that follows which brings about God's purpose for our life: to be saved, spirit-filled, sanctified, submissive "to Him" and to suffer "for Him." This is the mind of Christ for our lives, but it doesn't happen overnight. This is what Paul speaks to when he says we are continuously transformed by the renewing of our mind. I know you have heard it too many times, but how does one eat an elephant? One bite at a time.

God wants us to discover and discern our dependence on Him by determining that we cannot accomplish His purpose for our lives without Him and then deepening our relationship with and in Him through the transformation that comes by diluting ourselves and delving into His word. When believers grasp this concept and these principles, they become a force to be reckoned with. Not because of their own power but because they are now operating in the power of God. Nevertheless, be aware, Satan does not like this at all. So what does he do? Satan's game plan is to create strongholds in your life. He does this by utilizing a variety of falsities: false reality, false identity, false security, and false expectations. Let's look at each area individually and contrast truth with falsity.

False Reality – Reality means truth, certainty, veracity, authenticity and genuineness. It means the real thing. It means what's really going on or what's really happening. There is only one way to know what the real deal is, and that's through the revelation of the Holy Spirit to your mind. Satan knows that, so he will try to encourage you to call what you see your reality. After all, if you can see it and touch it, it must be real, right! Not always. Paul says in II Corinthians 5:7 –

For we walk by faith, not by sight.

Satan is the master of deception and he will make subtle changes to God's instructions that can be overlooked to the natural mind. The natural mind is not just the minds of unbelievers; it can also be an un-yielded mind of a believer. If you recall Satan's conversation with Eve in the garden, he made subtle changes in reference to what God told them and she was deceived.

> *And the woman said unto the serpent, We may eat of the fruit of the trees of the garden: ³But of the fruit of the tree which is in the midst of the garden, God hath said, Ye shall not eat of it, neither shall ye touch it, lest ye die. ⁴And the serpent said unto the woman, Ye shall not surely die: ⁵For God doth know that in the day ye eat thereof, then your eyes shall be opened, and ye shall be as gods, knowing good and evil.*

If false reality is replaced with false realism, it conveys a different meaning. False realism speaks to practicality, pragmatism and common sense. These meanings are significantly different than truth, certainty, veracity, authenticity and genuineness. But by the time you figure that out, he's accomplished his goal. It is much easier to misunderstand what's practical or what's common sense than it is to misunderstand the truth or what's authentic.

False Identity - Identity is defined as the consistent collective characteristics by which something is recognized or known. This definition is quite befitting for an unbeliever. The world will identify you with the things you do, the things you say, the places you go, the things you eat, etc. It may not be a true identity, but the worldview is based on shallow determinants. For believers, however, our identity is determined by God. Even if our outward portrayal shows flaws, that does not mean we are not who and what God says we are. We may not have matured to that level yet, but your God given identity is in there.

God knows who we are because He made us and created purpose in us. We come to know our identity and purpose through our relationship with God. This relationship is developed over time through prayer, study and fellowship with him and other believers. I'm about to go out on a limb, but I think it's a limb that will hold up: every person struggling with their identity is more than likely failing in at least one of these three areas as it relates to their relationship with God. Satan knows that we struggle with a consistent prayer life. He knows that too many believers are very weak in their bible study. He knows that we have become so busy that we don't share in the fellowship with God or other believers as we should.

In 2006, Baylor University and the Gallup Organization released results from a survey of Americans' religious habits. Their combined results revealed that "three-fourths of Americans pray at least once a week and more than one-fourth prayed several times a day" (*Lexington Herald-Leader*, Jan. 13, 2007). In addition, George Barna also says, "Christians spend seven times as much time on entertainment as they do on spiritual activities."

> Not as many people pray as we think they do.
>
> Not as many people pray as say they do.
>
> Those who don't have a dedicated daily prayer time, but say they pray all day, really don't.

Overall, it was concluded that an average Christian prays 3-7 minutes a day (including meal time prayers). With all that has happened in our world since 2006, do you think these numbers have gotten better or worse in 2012?

Either way, the bottom line is that believers must have an on-going consistent relationship with God through prayer, study and fellowship if they are to be strong and confident in their identity in Christ. Paul assures us in Romans 8 -

> *For whom he did foreknow, he also did predestinate to be conformed to the image of his Son, that he might be the firstborn among many*

brethren. Moreover whom he did predestinate, them he also called: and whom he called, them he also justified: and whom he justified, them he also glorified.

What shall we then say to these things? If God be for us, who can be against us?

Verses 29-31

Nay, in all these things we are more than conquerors through him that loved us. For I am persuaded, that neither death, nor life, nor angels, nor principalities, nor powers, nor things present, nor things to come, Nor height, nor depth, nor any other creature, shall be able to separate us from the love of God, which is in Christ Jesus our Lord.

Verses 37-39

False Security – Security is defined as freedom from risk or danger; safety. Freedom from doubt, anxiety, or fear; Confidence. Something that gives or assures safety. Something deposited or given as assurance of the fulfillment of an obligation or a pledge. This is what the believer has in Christ. His death, burial and resurrection make it so. This is also what makes Satan shake in his boots because even if the believer is not aware or assured in this, Satan knows it's true. Jesus said in John 10:27-29;

> *My sheep hear my voice, and I know them, and they follow me: And I give unto them eternal life; and they shall never perish, neither shall any man pluck them out of my hand. My Father, which gave them me, is greater than all; and no man is able to pluck them out of my Father's hand.*

Paul provides additional assurance of our security in Christ at Ephesians 4:30. The believer is sealed not until but unto the day of redemption.

> *And grieve not the Holy Spirit of God, whereby ye are sealed unto the day of redemption.*

After reading the passage above, you can see why Satan does not want the believer to be aware of the Blessed guarantee that he has in Christ, so he provides everything the immature believer needs to develop fear and doubt. This is what causes so many believers (non-believers also) to put their trust in weapons, gang affiliation, money, relationships and any other like thing, only to realize later that none of these assures security. Instead of trusting in these worldly pursuits, the believer should heed the advice offered in Proverbs 3:5-6;

> *Trust in the LORD with all thine heart; and lean not unto thine own understanding. In all thy ways acknowledge him, and he shall direct thy paths.*

We can also find strength, encouragement and security in the words of the apostle Peter,

> *Grace and peace be multiplied to you in the knowledge of God and of Jesus our Lord, as His divine power has given to us all things that pertain to life and godliness, through the knowledge of Him who called us by glory and virtue, by which have been given to us exceedingly great and precious promises, that through these you may be partakers of the divine nature, having escaped the corruption that is in the world through lust"*
>
> 2 Peter 1:2–4

> *Be careful for nothing; but in everything by prayer and supplication with thanksgiving let your requests be made known unto God.*
>
> Philippians 4:6

False Expectations – Expectation is defines as:

> The act or state of expecting or looking forward to an event as about to happen. That which is expected or looked for. The prospect of the future; grounds upon which something excellent is expected to occur.

I recall a conversation with my brother where the subject of unexpected telephone calls in the middle of the night surfaced. He said it's interesting that when it happens and someone is there with him, their thoughts are, "something bad has happened!" My brother's first thought is, "somebody has probably dialed my number in error. What is it that makes one person think alarm while another thinks calm? What is it that makes one person choose a negative response first and another a positive one first? What is it that makes one person choose pessimism and another person choose optimism? I think the answer is the peace of God as opposed to a piece of God. Isaiah 26:3 says,

> *Thou wilt keep him in perfect peace, whose mind is stayed on thee: because he trusteth in thee.*

I am not saying that optimists are never alarmed; they just have a pattern of taking the high road or thinking the better thought first.

Comparatively speaking, all of the Christian people I know and/or have ever met would not scratch the surface percentage wise if compared to the enormity of believers on this planet. Yet I would venture to say that many of the perceptions and expectations that they shared are probably consistent with many of yours. I want to list some for further discussion.

1. God knows my heart
2. Ain't nobody perfect.
3. There are people in all religions that are going to heaven.
4. If he is a Christian, I know I am.
5. If you have faith the size of a mustard seed, you can move mountains.
6. I can do anything I desire because I can do all things through Christ.
7. Resist the devil and he will flee.
8. I can name it and claim it. I can speak those things that be not, as though they be.
9. You can be healed of anything and everything if your faith is strong enough.

OK, I think that's enough. I'm sure you have heard these statements as I have. As noble and perceptive as these expectations may be, if they are tainted, they will not yield the intended result. You may remember that one of the definitions of expectation is, "The prospect of the future; grounds upon which something excellent is expected to occur." God has made some promises to us and God's promises are true. They cannot fail and He cannot lie. However, although there is some truth in some of the 9 statements I listed above, let's see how they line up with the word of God.

God does know our heart and He knows what's in our heart. Nevertheless, that does not provide us the opportunity to do as we please without consequences. David said,

> *Thy word have I hid in mine heart, that I might not sin against thee.*
>
> Psalms 199:11

> *Create in me a clean heart, O God; and renew a right spirit within me.*
>
> Psalms 51:10

> *For as he thinketh in his heart, so is he:*
>
> Proverbs 23:7

No there is none perfect as the world defines perfection, except Jesus Christ. However, Jesus tells us in Matthew 5:48,

> *Be ye therefore perfect, even as your Father which is in heaven is perfect.*

In I Peter 5:10 we are assured –

> *But the God of all grace, who hath called us unto his eternal glory by Christ Jesus, after that ye have suffered a while, make you perfect, stablish, strengthen, settle you.*

Lastly, consider Paul's words in Galatians 3:3,

> *Are ye so foolish? having begun in the Spirit, are ye now made perfect by the flesh?*

The thought that everyone from every religion can be on course for heaven is disingenuous. All religions don't accept Jesus Christ as Lord and Savior. If you are of the Christian persuasion you must have a relationship with Jesus Christ to be assured entrance into heaven, not a certain religion.

> *Jesus said, No man can come to me, except the Father which hath sent me draw him: and I will raise him up at the last day.*
>
> John 6:44

> *Jesus saith unto him, I am the way, the truth, and the life: no man cometh unto the Father, but by me.*
>
> John 14:6

Assurance of one's position with and in Christ is not based on comparisons to and with other people. All Christians are a work in progress; we make mistakes. If you focus on the actions or inactions of others, you will often find yourself on the wrong path. Jesus is the only reliable and acceptable example to follow.

> *Thy word is a lamp unto my feet, and a light unto my path.*
>
> Psalms 119:105

> *And he said to them all, If any man will come after me, let him deny himself, and take up his cross daily, and follow me.*
>
> Luke 9:23

I can move mountains if I have faith the size of a mustard seed. If you read what our Lord said about the mustard seed, He did not say size, He said as a grain of mustard seed.

> *And Jesus said unto them, Because of your unbelief: for verily I say unto you, If ye have faith as a grain of mustard seed, ye shall say unto this*

> mountain, Remove hence to yonder place; and it shall remove; and nothing shall be impossible unto you.
>
> Matthew 17:20
>
> It is like a grain of mustard seed, which a man took, and cast into his garden; and it grew, and waxed a great tree; and the fowls of the air lodged in the branches of it.
>
> Luke 13:19

Satan wants you to think size; small faith, little faith, little results. Jesus never promoted little faith. In fact, He said on more than one occasion "O ye of little faith" and He was not pleased in these instances. The greater message here is, as little or small as we might think our faith is in any given situation, exercise it because the power is not in the faith but in the one your faith is in, Jesus Christ. If we maintain that focus, we too will see tiny seeds planted and great trees yielded and like the fowls of the air lodging in the mustard tree, people will find comfort in the branches our faith produces. Nothing will be impossible to the one that trusts in the Lord and operates in His will.

Too many have misread the passage at Philippians 4:13. They understand it to say because they are believers, they can do all things; heal any condition, win any battle, basically, succeed in any endeavor they choose. However, again, this is not the message Paul is sending.

You can read the entire chapter, but I selected verses 6-8 and 12-13 to clarify Paul's point.

> *Be careful for nothing; but in everything by prayer and supplication with thanksgiving let your requests be made known unto God.*
>
> *And the peace of God, which passeth all understanding, shall keep your hearts and minds through Christ Jesus.*
>
> *Finally, brethren, whatsoever things are true, whatsoever things are honest, whatsoever things are just, whatsoever things are pure, whatsoever things are lovely, whatsoever things are of good report; if there be any virtue, and if there be any praise, think on these things.*
>
> *I know both how to be abased, and I know how to abound: everywhere and in all things I am instructed both to be full and to be hungry, both to abound and to suffer need.*
>
> *I can do all things through Christ which strengtheneth me.*

Paul is saying to the Philippians people that although you don't have to be cautious or timid about your ministry, let prayer and supplication with thanksgiving motivate your request to God. God will keep and guide your thoughts through Christ Jesus. Focus on things that are just, pure, lovely, of good report, virtuous and praise-worthy. He tells them that personally, he has practiced this method and has found peace within it. It is after properly positioning oneself in this way that the statement in verse 13 reflects its true intent. I can endure all things through the help and direction of Christ because in Him is my strength.

If I resist the devil, he will flee from me. Although this is part of the verse recorded at James 4:7, I would not encourage anyone to apply this portion alone if the expectation is to put the devil at flight. This may deflate some egos, but without the power of Jesus Christ, we cannot chase the devil away. Jesus is not only our model, He is also our Great Warrior. The passage in its entirety says,

> *Submit yourselves therefore to God. Resist the devil, and he will flee from you.*

The key here is the submitting to God. In the 4th chapter of Matthew, Satan was bold enough to even challenge Jesus. It goes without question that he will challenge you and me. Jesus didn't simply say, "I resist you devil," and he fled. No Jesus submitted unto God as well. He said, It is written. If we are going to be successful in our challenges with the devil, we too will have to use the same example. We must know the word of God if we are to use it. Then we begin to use our minds to apply the word, which utilizes the power of God to cause the devil to flee.

I can name it and claim it; I can speak those things that be not, as though they be. Who is in control anyway? I think about God's reply to Job in the 38th chapter of the same book.

> Then the LORD answered Job out of the whirlwind, and said,
>
> Where wast thou when I laid the foundations of the earth? declare, if thou hast understanding.
>
> Job 38:1&4

God has given man a measure of creative power (Gen 2:19 and 11:4-5);

> And out of the ground the LORD God formed every beast of the field, and every fowl of the air; and brought them unto Adam to see what he would call them: and whatsoever Adam called every living creature, that was the name thereof.
>
> And they said, Go to, let us build us a city and a tower, whose top may reach unto heaven; and let

> *us make us a name, lest we be scattered abroad upon the face of the whole earth. And the LORD came down to see the city and the tower, which the children of men builded.*

However, there are limitations to it. First of all, everything that man creates is made from a substance or substances that God already created. Secondly, God looks at the intended use of man's creation and exercises His sovereign right to allow it, alter it, prevent it or destroy it. Whatever decision He makes is the right one. We cannot dictate to God what He must do. If we could, what would happen when two people declared two opposing requests: you declare wealth for my life and I declare poverty for my life. Silly example, but what happens? I know, God decides; He always does.

> *Hath not the potter power over the clay, of the same lump to make one vessel unto honour, and another unto dishonour?*
>
> Romans 9:21

You can be healed of anything and everything if your faith is strong enough. There was an occasion in the gospel of Mark where Jesus performed a healing that His disciples could not.

> *And when he was come into the house, his disciples asked him privately, Why could not we cast him out?*
>
> *And he said unto them, This kind can come forth by nothing, but by prayer and fasting.*
>
> Mark 9:28-29

Also, in the gospel of John, there was a blind man from birth that Jesus healed.

> *And as Jesus passed by, he saw a man which was blind from his birth.*
>
> *And his disciples asked him, saying, Master, who did sin, this man, or his parents, that he was born blind?*
>
> *Jesus answered, Neither hath this man sinned, nor his parents: but that the works of God should be made manifest in him.*
>
> John 9:1-3

Since the focus of this chapter is on the "Mind" to be, let me appeal to the mind. Jesus said to the disciples in Mark's account, "This kind can come forth by nothing, but by prayer and fasting." Jesus didn't fast or pray before casting out the demon; He just spoke and it was done. In the account recorded in the gospel of John,

Jesus told His disciples that sin didn't cause the blindness, it happened so that the glory of God would be revealed.

If everybody was healed of every illness, disease, pain and/or life threatening condition, people would never die. This might sound like heaven, but with our present bodies decaying daily and falling apart, what quality of life would that be? If every condition could be healed with only a certain amount of faith being the determinant, the apostle Paul should have been at the top of the healing list. Yet we know he was never healed of his condition. Instead, God provided him sufficient grace. If we closely examine the word of God, I believe we will find that first of all, it is God that heals; not faith. Secondly, as we discovered earlier, God chooses. Sometimes He heals, sometimes He provides sufficient grace to endure it, and sometimes He takes us to our heavenly home.

Without question there is an enormous amount of scriptural support that the bible provides to properly address these particular statements and more. If what I have provided does not convince you, by all means further study is warranted. I encourage you to do so. Satan delights in the unknown or uncertain areas of our Christian walk. Conversely, if this information has provided new light where there was darkness, walk boldly in this new understanding.

We must always remember that;

> **God is our reality**, For in him we live, move and have our being.
>
> Acts 17:28,
>
> **God is our identity**, I am a new creation because I am in Christ.
>
> 2Corinthians 5:17,
>
> **God is our security**; I am always in the presence of God because He never leaves me.
>
> Hebrews 13:5,
>
> **God is our expectation**; I have been given exceedingly great and precious promises by God by which I share His nature.
>
> 2 Peter 1:4
>
> **And,**
> I am seated in heavenly places with Christ.
>
> Eph 2:6

If I were to borrow a practice from my Pastor, I would take the "R" from reality, the "I" from identity, the "S" from security and the "E" from expectations and present the word RISE. That is what God wants from us; He wants us to yield our minds to Him so we can rise above the deceptive gimmicks that Satan uses to control our minds.

As I come to the conclusion of not only this chapter but this book as well, I want to draw your attention back to my purpose for writing. As believers, we need to know God's will for our lives, and we need to know that the process involves ups and downs, right and wrongs, successes and failures, but we can't allow the bondage of a legalistic perspective to control our minds. James Montgomery Boice wrote in his book, *Renewing Your Mind in a Mindless World* – "Christians often get greatly hung up on the idea of discovering what God's specific will is for their lives." The book's basis comes from Romans 12:2. God's will is all about sacrifice, service and reward. Boice says, "He is no fool who gives away what he cannot keep to gain what he cannot lose."

Bishop Paul S. Morton points out in *The Enemy Inside Your Mind*, "There has to be a starting point and for believers." It is to examine our beliefs, our feelings, and our behavior based on the teachings of the eternal and unfailing word of God. We have thoughts in our minds that have been recorded and kept there throughout our lifetime. They are untrue but we believe them because we have heard them repeated so many times that our mind replays them over and over almost automatically. Through the power of the mind we can not only recall the past; we can actually relive it. Whether good or bad, some people choose to live their current lives like it is actually 5, 10, 20, maybe even 30 years ago. The mind is just that powerful.

If you are honest with yourself, you can hear a song from years ago and instantly remember where you were, who you were with and maybe some other things as well.

Finally, my objective in this work was not to minimize or diminish the importance of what we as believers "do." James 1:22 says, "But be doers of the word, and not hearers only, deceiving yourselves." Here, doing is contrasted with hearing. I am speaking to the importance of "being." What you are determines what you do but the reverse is not true. A bee stings because it is the nature of a bee; however, every sting does not originate from a bee.

My objective has been to provide assurance that God has a specific will and purpose for your life. Discovering it involves a process: to be saved, spirit-filled, sanctified, submissive "to Him," and to suffer "for Him." God has a purpose, a call, a place, a decision, a challenge, a need, a certain way and a certain mind or mind-set for all of us. Lastly, we must guard our minds because God has given us powerful minds that were intended to be used by Him and for Him. If you are able to accept that, "This is the Mind to Be." *To Be, or Not To Be*, I am convinced, "That Is The Question."

www.ingramcontent.com/pod-product-compliance
Lightning Source LLC
Chambersburg PA
CBHW070640050426
42451CB00008B/243